Editorial Director: Jonathan Leeman
Managing Editor: Taylor Hartley
Editors: Alex Duke and David Daniels
Copy Editor: Judith Henderson
Executive Director: Ryan Townsend
President: Mark Dever
Cover Design: Odd Notion
Layout Design: Rubner Durais
Paperback ISBN: 979-8-89218-109-9

Church Matters: Seasons in a Pastor's Life
Copyright © 2024 by 9Marks
All rights reserved. No part of this publication may be reproduced, stored in a retrieval system, or transmitted in any form by any means, electronic, mechanical, photocopy, recording, or otherwise, without the prior permission of 9Marks, except as provided for by USA copyright law.

Scripture quotations are from the ESV® Bible (The Holy Bible, English Standard Version®), copyright © 2001 by Crossway, a publishing ministry of Good News Publishers. Used by permission. All rights reserved.
All emphases in Scripture quotations have been added by the author.

Tools like this are provided by the generous investment of donors.
Each gift to 9Marks helps equip church leaders with a biblical vision and practical resources for displaying God's glory to the nations through healthy churches.

Donate at: www.9marks.org/donate.
Or make checks payable to "9Marks" and mail to:
    9 Marks
    525 A St. NE
    Washington, DC 20002

info@9marks.org | www.9marks.org

More Resources from 9Marks

For more information, visit **9marks.org**.

10   Editor's Note
     by Jonathan Leeman

At the Starting Blocks: Preparation

14   Join a Church and Follow a Faithful Pastor
     by Joshua Chatman

17   Elder Before You Elder
     by Zack DiPrima

21   Attend to Your Character
     by Garrett Conner

24   Listen to Others More Than Yourself: The External Call
     by V. Samuel Clintoc

27   Balance Patience and Ambition
     by Billy Dalton

31   You Aspire, but Are You Willing?
     by Raymond Johnson

34   Candidate Wisely and Honestly
     by Branton Burleson

After the Gun: First Five Years

40   Find a Mentor!
     by Cheston Pickard

43   Be a Strong and Courageous Young Leader
     by Clint Darst

46   Patience! Pick Your Battles Wisely
     by Jeramie Rinne

50   Loving Your Family While Leading God's Church
     by Liam Garvie

53   Take Heart: Preaching to Encourage
     by Tiago Oliveira

56   Young Pastor, Care for the Older Members of Your Flock
     by Dave Kiehn

59   Make the Main Thing the Main Thing on Sundays
     by Bret Capranica

62	Creating Healthy Membership Practices *by Jon Deedrick*
67	Unique Temptations for a New Pastor *by Brian Parks*

Over the Long Haul: The Middle Years

72	Prepare for Unexpected Storms *by Josh Manley*
75	Raise up Leaders *by John Folmar*
79	Persevere in the Highs and Lows *by Clift Barnes*
82	Every Week I Preach My Guts out and . . . Nothing Changes *by David King*
85	Work Hard and Stay Hungry *by Juan Sanchez*

Passing the Baton: Transitioning to the Next Guy

90	How to Decide When It's Time to Stay or Go *by Phil Newton*
94	Why Is It Hard for Pastors to Let Go? *by Sandy Willson*
97	Plan Your Transition *by Michael Indorf*
101	Preparing a Church for Pastoral Transition *by William Spink, Jr.*
104	Support the Next Guy *by Doug Van Meter*
107	How Should I Serve My Church after I Stop Being Its Senior Pastor? *by Bob Johnson*

Finishing the Race

112   Six Lessons I Learned When I Could Not Pastor
by John Erickson

116   Learn to Rest
by Wes Pastor

119   Pastor, Remember Where Your Identity Is Found Before You Retire
by Phil Newton

123   Brothers, Train up the Next Generation
by Mike Bullmore

126   Anticipating Your Reward
by Omar Johnson

Biblical Thinking For

Building
Healthy
Churches

Editor's Note

by Jonathan Leeman

Recently I had lunch with a friend whose wife is midway through cancer treatment. I wondered if her cancer is the central feature of his daily life, the hub around which every other logistic and emotion turned. He said it is. It impacts his job, his day-to-day activities, his children's lives, their ability to attend church, everything. A predominate theme in our conversation was life seldom looks like you expect it to look.

When you're young, you expect things like marriage and career to look one way, but so often it looks different. Like walking around the Byzantine hallways of a sprawling shopping mall, you sometimes stop, look around, and think, "Wait, how did I get here? Where am I?"

So in the life of a pastor. Entering the pastorate, you have one set of expectations. Then ministry takes you down strange pathways, whole seasons you didn't anticipate. Every once in a while, you look around and think, "How did we get here? And, goodness, I'm tired."

Having folks one or two steps ahead is helpful for moving through different seasons. They can explain what to expect. Satan fools us into thinking our situation is unique, our temptations unusual, our exhaustion beyond reckoning, like lions isolating an antelope from the herd. Yet how reassuring for an older brother to come along, place an arm around the shoulder, and say, "Don't worry. I was there. And I got through it. Here's what God taught me." Ah, yes, maybe I can make it through, too.

Our goal for this edition of *Church Matters* is to have a number of men offer that arm for the shoulder. What should you expect for getting started, for the early stages of the race, for the many laps which follow, and for gliding gracefully through the finish line? Different seasons impose different challenges and afford different opportunities. Brother pastor, are you ready for the next season?

I turned fifty last September. It gave me the opportunity to stop and reflect on the timeline of my life and its seasons. Mostly, I feel gratitude for all that God has given. Yet one thing a man generally possesses at fifty that he does not possess at thirty is a stronger sense of his limitations and weaknesses. More and more I find myself thinking, "Lord, just help me to make it to the end in good shape."

Then I read Mike Bullmore's piece. He might call this Hezekiah-think. Hezekiah, you might remember, was happy the kingdom of Israel would be spared in his lifetime, never mind what happened after him.

Have I been succumbing to one temptation common to pastors and elders somewhere in the middle of their race, the temptation to fight just hard enough to preserve yourself, but maybe not hard enough to build the next generation?

We pray this edition of *Church Matters* might help you to discern where you're at, so that you might better prepare for what's ahead.

Jonathan Leeman edits all 9Marks titles as well as *Church Matters*. He is the author of several books focusing on ecclesiology. Jonathan earned his MDiv from Southern Seminary and a Ph.D. in Ecclesiology from the University of Wales. He lives with his wife and four daughters in Cheverly, Maryland, where he is an elder at Cheverly Baptist Church.

Section One

At the Starting Blocks: Preparation

Join a Church and Follow a Faithful Pastor

by Joshua Chatman

Attempting to run a marathon without any proper training would be foolish, and possibly deadly. Your mind, legs, and lungs are not able to run that type of distance naturally.

To pursue pastoral ministry without proper training would be even more detrimental to yourself and others.

That training could include seminary. However, there are two components more vital than seminary to ministry preparation—joining a church and following faithful pastors.

You may think these go without saying, yet they need to be stated and restated. The training that comes from joining a church and following faithful pastors is invaluable and irreplaceable.

Joining a Local Church

The New Testament is clear: identifying with Christ necessarily includes identifying with his people (Matt. 16:18, Acts 2:47, Heb. 10:24–25). The church is the family of God—the new covenant community. In aspiring to be a leader within this family, you must first join the family, which is formalized through church membership.

> "The training that comes from joining a church and following faithful pastors is invaluable and irreplaceable."

Joining before leading is common sense. Apart from joining a church, you'll have nothing more than assumptions about how the church functions and lives as a local body. You learn so much within the church that shapes how you would lead a church.

As a member, aspiring pastors experience how the church weeps and rejoices together (Rom. 12:15). They're trained to humble themselves and submit to leaders and fellow members (Heb. 13:17, Eph. 5:19). They see what it looks like to labor to fulfill the Great Commission.

Joining a church is also essential because brothers are to be exemplary members prior to serving as pastors. A pastor is more than a church member, yet they're not less than one. The qualifications of an elder assume he is to be a model member before being installed as an elder (1 Tim. 3:1–7).

Aspiring pastors, then, must do the work of pastoring long before they become pastors. They must labor for the maturity of the church, serve their brothers and sisters (Rom. 12:9–11, 1 Pet. 4:9–11), look to the interests of others (Phil. 2:1–5), speak the truth in love (Eph. 4:15–16), bear burdens (Gal. 6:2), maintain unity eagerly (Eph. 4:1–3), encourage straying and struggling sheep (Heb. 3:12–13), and prioritize the gathering (Heb. 10:24–25).

The longer one is a faithful member of a faithful church, the more prepared he is to pastor.

Following Faithful Pastors

Scripture mandates that members follow their pastors' faith and life (Heb. 13:7). Following faithful pastors in your local church allows you to learn from those who are seasons ahead and get a window into the work you aspire to do someday. Without this, you can have a romanticized view of pastoral ministry—like assuming it only consists of sermon preparation, or that pastors are spiritual CEOs. Following a good man will quickly debunk and correct wrong assumptions.

In theater, the director ensures that the main character has an understudy, a person who is able to act as a replacement if necessary. The understudy shadows the lead character, learning his or her lines, following moves, and asking questions. The more the understudy observes, the more he or she is prepared.

In spending time with faithful pastors, aspiring pastors observe how to prepare sermons, pray for church members, equip the saints for the work of ministry, minister to struggling sheep, pursue straying sheep, conduct weddings and funerals, lead elders' meetings, and

> "The longer one is a faithful member of a faithful church, the more prepared he is to pastor."

more. These opportunities are invaluable and available to the one who chooses to take advantage of them. You witness in real time what you read about in books, and it pays dividends in the long run.

The saying holds true, "More things are caught than taught." Paul could speak so highly of Timothy's character and competence because Timothy spent so much time following Paul and ministering alongside him (1 Thes. 3:1–6, Phil. 2:19–22, 1 Tim. 1:3–4, 2 Tim. 3:10–11).

When you reach miles ten, fifteen, and twenty in a marathon, you know what to do because—if you're wise—you've trained for it. In pastoral ministry, prior prioritization of church membership and following faithful pastors provides experience that will help you persevere to the finish line.

Joshua Chatman is a pastor of Midtown Baptist Church in Memphis, Tennessee.

Elder Before You Elder

by Zack DiPrima

The office of pastor isn't the birthright of the aspirational. Wanting to be a pastor doesn't make you one. The office of pastor (elder, shepherd, overseer) is a calling given from the risen Christ to be recognized by local churches. A congregation must affirm what God has done to prepare a man to shepherd God's people.[1]

Many men experience a long onramp to formal pastoral ministry. For some, this can be a discouraging time, waiting for what feels like the glacial approval of a skeptical congregation. I would discourage such discouragement. Proper preparation will profoundly serve your ministry in the long run—and can be a great joy in the meantime.

The question remains: what should an aspiring elder do until he's recognized as an elder? The answer is simple. He should *elder* before he elders. He should *shepherd* before he shepherds. He should actively exhibit the ordinary qualities of a faithful pastor before he is officially recognized as one. Below are just a few ways to do so.

Cultivate Communion with God

This is not an article about holiness. Nevertheless, the indispensability of a pastor's piety cannot be overstated. Indeed, there's no more practical way for a pastor to serve his congregation than through his own pursuit of godliness. This is why Robert Murray M'Cheyne (1813–1843) once told a friend, "It is not great talents God blesses so much as great likeness to Jesus. A holy minister is an awful weapon in the hand of God."[2]

M'Cheyne understood that the greatest need of a man's future congregation is his own communion with God. Deep friendship with Christ and true usefulness in the kingdom are inseparable. This means aspiring pastors serve others *from their own pursuit of holiness*. Andrew Bonar wrote of M'Cheyne,

> From the first he fed others by what he himself was feeding upon. His preaching was in a manner the development of his soul's experience. It was a giving out of the inward life. He loved to come up from the pastures wherein the Chief Shepherd had met him—to lead the flock entrusted to his care to the spots where he found nourishment.[3]

The great task of a pastor is to lead sheep to the Great Shepherd. And the best pastor is the man who leads the flock along the same path he has tread time and time again.

Yet leading others to Christ is not a practice limited to pastors. If you're an aspiring minister, every encounter with a church member provides a fresh opportunity to feed others out of the abundance of your own walk with God. Every greeting, every conversation, every email, every text message, every sermon, every devotional is a prime opportunity to share from the storehouse of your own experience of knowing God.

Do Everything Pastorally

When preparing to become an elder, preaching and public teaching opportunities are not the only ways to display the character of a godly elder. Rather, good shepherds are always shepherding. There's a way to welcome visitors *pastorally*. There's a way to email parents about the upcoming youth event *pastorally*. There's a way to coordinate Sunday morning greeters *pastorally*. There's a way to encourage and exhort an A/V volunteer *pastorally*. There's a way to grab coffee with a new Christian *pastorally*. There's a way to give announcements, pray publicly, and lead elements of a worship service *pastorally*. Each of these examples provides an opportunity to flex pastoral muscles and do spiritual good to others.

Pursue Public Virtue

Christians are right to prioritize private character over public. Indeed, there's a type of performative virtue that Jesus condemns (Matt. 6:5–6). However, the character of a pastor must always be evident and obvious. The entire point of the elder qualifications in the pastoral epistles is for congregations to *notice* the character of aspiring officers.

This means it's not enough for a young man to be able to teach—he must demonstrate his ability. It's not enough for a young man to be hospitable—he must show hospitality. It's not enough for a young man to be gentle—he must be known for gentleness. Even Timothy—who was already serving in a pastoral role and had received a glowing endorsement from the apostle Paul—was called to pursue pastoral virtue "so that all may see [his] progress" (1 Tim. 4:15).

It's often the case that younger men can quickly prove their ability to teach, but they struggle to convey warmth and affection for the people of God. They may truly love their church, but it's not always obvious in their tone and manner. It's much easier to prove mastery of the text you're preaching than love for the people you're addressing. "Getting the text right" is non-negotiable. But conveying love for the congregation as you preach is just as much a priority (1 Cor. 13). The aspiring pastor should resolve that his love for the congregation is never questioned.

Another pastoral qualification young men tend to neglect is respectability (1 Tim. 3:2), and they therefore fail to earn the trust of older men.

When a man becomes a pastor, he's called to shepherd the whole flock. He must be capable of providing soul care to the young, the middle-aged, and the elderly. If you're an aspiring pastor, I encourage you to ask yourself the following questions, "Do I show spiritual care for the generations older than me? Do I struggle to earn the trust of older people in the flock? Would the fifty-year-old man in my church trust me to care for his soul? What about the souls of his wife and children? Are there any aspects of my lifestyle or the way I present myself that erect barriers to earning the respect of older members?"

> "It's much easier to prove mastery of the text you're preaching than love for the people you're addressing."

Young men should remove roadblocks to respectability. This may affect the way they dress. It may affect how or whether they employ generational slang in their sermons. It may affect their priorities, their tone, and how they use their time. Every church is located in a cultural context, and a young man needs to be aware of his context, lest he carelessly puts stumbling blocks in people's way in non-essential matters (1 Cor. 8:9). Paul said, "Let no one despise you for your youth, but set the believers an example in speech, in conduct, in love, in faith, in purity" (1 Tim. 4:12). This means that older generations should not discount a man sheerly because of his age. But it also means young men should not present unnecessary obstacles to earning the approval of seasoned saints.

Conclusion

Aspiring ministers can't do everything an elder can do. But they can love and care for the people of God in meaningful ways. Nothing prevents them from growing in godliness and exhibiting pastoral character privately and publicly. Every church needs men who do the work of pastoring before they're officially recognized as pastors.

1. Caleb Morell, "Do Elders Receive Their Authority by Congregational Vote?" 9Marks. August 19, 2022. https://www.9marks.org/article/do-elders-receive-their-authority-by-congregational-vote/.

2. Andrew Bonar, The Memoir and Remains of the Rev. Robert Murray M'Cheyne (Carlisle, PA: Banner of Truth Trust), 282.

3. Bonar, Memoir and Remains, 36.

Zack DiPrima is a teaching elder of Trinity Church Kennesaw in Kennesaw, Georgia.

Attend to Your Character

by Garrett Conner

"It is notoriously the case that the outward life of a minister (like the life of any professing Christian) can look one way and the inner reality be substantially different." – Robert Yarbrough[1]

Before I entered the pastorate, I had marks of Christian character that brothers saw as commendable—hard-working, eager for coaching, zealous for the local church. I loved to hear the Word and to evangelize. My character, however, was lacking.

In those early days of ministry preparation, I needed discipling. I needed an older man to address my decision-making, dating habits, stewardship, and spiritual disciplines. At 21 years old, I pridefully assumed that my shortcomings would iron themselves out over time.

In 1 Timothy 4:16, Paul assumes Timothy's character will have a tangible impact on the fruitfulness of his ministry. The apostle said, "Pay close attention *to your life* and your teaching; persevere in these things, for in doing this, you will save both yourself and your hearers."

Our character can be used by God for eternal good—or our lack thereof can wreak havoc. For the sake of you and your future people's souls, here are three simple ways to attend to your character.

Believe Jesus Loves You

Sometimes, the most prideful people can be pastors. Pride is known for self-promotion and humble brags. But sometimes, there is a stealth-like pride that manifests as self-loathing. It ignores the humbling truth of Jesus's love in favor of our own foolish introspection and self-comparison.

Our pride and unbelief cause us to forget that God loves us and rejoices over us in Christ. I encourage you to start telling yourself that God is for you. Take this to heart: "God proves his own love for us in that while we were still sinners, Christ died for us" (Rom. 5:8).

The world, the flesh, and the devil remind me of how unlovely I am in my sin. It's true. But this dark backdrop makes the love of God shine in high definition. He loved us while we were enemies. He gave you his Holy Spirit, in love, to help you, even now. Meditate on these truths daily, brother.

Cultivate Private Worship

Since I was a child, I have always had problems with focus, but I can testify that God has worked amazing changes in my life by communing with him. Here are some practices to consider for your own edification.

Focus

I had a roommate in seminary named Peter who encouraged me to ask God for grace to focus. I started to remove distractions and things that were not good for my soul. For example, I needed less secular music, media, and news. I needed more songs of praise, Scripture, and prayer. I needed more time with Jesus. And the longer I pastor, the more I need.

Read

Years ago, an old friend and pastor named Bob encouraged me to read through the Bible with him in a year. I haven't stopped. There is nothing like repeatedly immersing yourself in the storyline of Scripture. Spurgeon said, "A Bible that is falling apart usually belongs to someone who isn't." Delight over the Word with a fellow church member.

Journal

Another friend, Dominic, encouraged me to journal my prayers. I was hesitant to try, but this has been one of the most life-changing and spiritually strengthening exercises for life and ministry. It has helped me focus, be more thoughtful in my communion with God, and deepen my love for him. It has forced me to sit down, examine my sin, and remember God's promises in the gospel.

> "Our character can be used by God for eternal good—or our lack thereof can wreak havoc."

Sing

Fill your life with good Christian music. Exalt God and exult in God. Pull back from songs that are of the flesh and grieve the Spirit. As you lift your hands in praise to God in private, he gives you renewed strength to fight sin.

Pursue Deep Discipleship

When I was in school, I was more involved with my church's ministries than discipling. I didn't know to ask someone to disciple me. I certainly wanted more coaching and personal involvement, but back then, "discipling" was not the buzzword it is today.

I badly needed someone to teach me how to mortify besetting sins like self-comparison, self-pity, lust, bitterness, and escapism. These sins are never fun to unearth. They humiliate us and cause us to shrink back. Nevertheless, Jesus did not come for the healthy, did he?

Maturity comes with knowing you need to grow in sanctification constantly. And God uses few things to grow us like relationships in a local church. Sadly, some men get degrees from seminaries but have a very weak relationship with a local church, if any at all. The irony is they expect to lead a church while they themselves have never submitted to one.

My counsel to those of you in training is to find a devoted pastor and involve him in your life. Ask him to run a diagnostic test on your personal habits and thought life. If single, converse with him about your dating. If married, then request that he ask you about your marriage and parenting. You also need encouragement when you are faithful, and a good pastor will be an encourager. This kind of relationship will grow your character and teach you how to be a better pastor one day.

May the Lord richly bless you in your time of training.[2]

---

1. Robert W. Yarbrough, *The Letters to Timothy and Titus,* ed. D. A. Carson, Pillar New Testament Commentary (Grand Rapids, MI; London: William B. Eerdmans Publishing Company; Apollos, 2018), 254.

2. *Recommended resources:* Dangerous Calling *by Paul David Tripp,* Character Matters *by Aaron Menikoff,* The Pillars of Christian Character *by John MacArthur, and* The Path to Being a Pastor *by Bobby Jamieson*

Garrett Conner is the senior pastor of La Plata Baptist Church in La Plata, Maryland.

Listen to Others More Than Yourself: The External Call

by V. Samuel Clintoc

Considering the call to pastor is a weighty matter. It should not be done superficially or individualistically.

In our society, where desires, feelings, and self-impressions are authoritative, it is tempting to anchor the call to ministry primarily in our self-assessment. Christians want to point to some "spiritual" experience, perhaps invoking the precedent of Paul's apostolic calling (Gal. 1:1, 16–17). But is this prudent?

The calling into the apostolic office was unique to the apostles and not prescriptive for subsequent generations of ministry calling.[1] Furthermore, the New Testament presents evidence of corporate responsibility in affirming one's call to ministry. Thus, my aim here is to persuade you to place greater weight on the evaluation of others than your own.

Why Listen to Others More Than to Yourself?

While the desire to serve as a pastor is good (1 Tim. 3:5), it is not sufficient ground, all by itself, to validate God's call upon someone for at least two reasons.

First, a church must assess and confirm a man's qualification before installing him in the pastoral office (1 Tim. 3:1–7, Titus 1:5–9). Clearly implied is that someone's call to ministry must be assessed and confirmed *by others*. Paul even cautions Timothy not to be "hasty in the laying on of hands" (1 Tim. 5:22).

Second, God himself involves others to publicly affirm calls to ministry, such as in Acts 13:2–3:

> While they were worshiping the Lord and fasting, the Holy Spirit said, "Set apart for me Barnabas and Saul for the work to which I have called them." Then after fasting and praying they laid their hands on them and sent them off.

It was the Holy Spirit's idea to have the church of Antioch set apart Paul and Barnabas. The calling of the Holy Spirit, therefore, does not bypass the church's public affirmation of ministry calling, but enables it. As Calvin said, "What was the purpose of that setting apart and laying on of hands after the Holy Spirit attested his choice, except to preserve church discipline in designating ministers through men?"[2]

Therefore, consider listening to others more than to yourself because the "external call" is the Holy Spirit's means to publicly affirm and reassure us of his calling. Such corporate affirmation of God's calling proves to be essential when we need encouragement to press on amid difficulties (2 Tim. 1:6–7).

How to Listen to Others Concerning Your Calling

Listen with Intentionality

Initiate! Tell your pastors how your heart is wrestling with your sense of calling to pastoral ministry. Ask for resources to read and discuss with them.[3] Invite them to pray for you, observe you, and speak into your life on this matter.

There are some traps to avoid here. Don't confuse intentionality with entitlement. That is, don't demand to be observed by the elders, nor come with a sense of having arrived and expect the elders must now give you public ministry opportunities. Instead, let them know of how you are wrestling and follow their lead and pace.

Listen with Humility

There is a prideful way to listen to others, namely, to get their approval. Instead, combine intentionality with humility. Listen to learn about yourself and not merely to be affirmed. Go in without any preconceived answers you hope to hear.

It's easy to let your identity or worth be wrapped up in your aspiration for pastoral ministry. We often have blind spots in assessing our own abilities or readiness, feeling wiser than we really are (Rom. 12:16b). Let others speak to you with candor, even if that means hearing about your shortcomings or unreadiness.

Listen with Patience

Remember how Moses waited several decades in obscurity before his ministry picked up traction. Don't circumvent the process by lacking patience. It's possible to ask for confirmation too hastily or abruptly. If your church is slow in affirming your calling, it's not wasted time. It might be God's way of testing if you will submit to his leading.

Who to Listen to as You Assess Your Calling

Listen to Your Wife

God has given you a wife to be your helper. So seek her help! You want all the wisdom she has. What's her assessment of you, your gifts, your character, and the opportunities in front of you? Then *listen* to her answers, don't try to *steer* them in the direction you want her to go. Trust that she is the gift God has given you to help discern his calling for your life.

Listen to Mature Believers

Hopefully you have around you several mature believers who know you well. Some might even be part of your family. Would any of them be positively or negatively surprised to hear that you are considering the call to ministry? Ask them why or why not.

Listen to Your Local Church

Do members of your church offer unsolicited feedback regarding the fruitfulness of how you serve them and handle God's Word, at least in personal conversations or small teaching roles? A congregation of believers should be able to observe your godliness and giftedness in ministering to others.

Listen to Your Pastors

While it's helpful to listen to church members or people who know you well, you should prioritize listening to those who also know the ministry well. They know the various facets of pastoral ministry and the burdens that belong to it. Hopefully you are in a church where the pastors have a healthy and robust understanding of their office.

Engage them early in the process of discerning God's call. Allow them time to observe you. Don't reach out only when you need them to write that reference letter for a seminary application. Offer to be a pastoral intern (even if unpaid) so you can be closer to your pastors and better observed.

The bottom line is, the call to ministry is not merely a self-assessment or individual decision; God designed his church to be involved in publicly affirming those whom he calls to the pastoral office, so listen to them more than to yourself.

---

1. *Calvin,* Institutes, 4.3.14
2. Institutes 4.3.14
3. *e.g. Charles Bridges,* The Christian Ministry, *especially part II, chapter 6*

V. Samuel Clintoc is a pastor of Park Hills Baptist Church in Austin, Texas.

Balance Patience and Ambition

by Billy Dalton

"I know this is disappointing to hear, but you are not ready to be in pastoral ministry."

This is one of the hardest things I periodically have to tell men aspiring to be pastors. I believe it is also the kindest thing I can say to save the men, their families, and their future congregations great heartache and pain. "Faithful are the wounds of a friend" (Prov. 27:6).

Churches must train the ambitious patiently, giving them time to show their true colors.

Places and Spaces

Places and spaces must be made to have hard conversations about ministry readiness. The aforementioned men had committed themselves to a season of training at our church, but during their preparation, issues

> "Churches must train the ambitious patiently, giving them time to show their true colors."

surfaced that temporarily or permanently disqualified them from pastoral ministry.

For some, character qualities emerged that conflicted with 1 Timothy 3 and Titus 1. Others did not yet know their Bibles well enough to rightly divide it and defend the faith against false doctrine. A number who did know their Bible well needed more practice and life experience to be able to teach and communicate effectively.

In a few instances, places and spaces revealed deep-seated habitual sins and ungodly motives for ministry. Whatever the situation, the hard conversation of readiness must come. Part of pastoral ministry is providing the space to make that happen.

The Church Is Your Friend

The adage "you don't know what you don't know" rings true in pastoral ministry. I have heard many brothers say they regret not having more time for preparation, especially to handle ministry issues that seminary or Bible college do not or cannot teach you.

Formal theological education is a good supplement, but pastoral preparation must happen in the local church. Men need the opportunity to have "on the job training" with real pastors in real situations. Many issues, questions, and scenarios will arise during this life-on-life training season that will teach the aspiring pastor there is a lot he does not know.

Certainly, no one will be completely ready for ministry or have all the answers before they start. We should grow throughout our ministries (2 Tim. 2:15). Yet the Lord has given the gift of his church to help men know when they are qualified to pastor.

Time Is Your Friend

Time gives opportunity to see how an aspiring brother will respond to a vast array of situations. Anyone can fake readiness for a short season. When given enough time, a person's true self comes out.

The apostle Paul exhorts us to be patient and let time do its revealing work by Word and Spirit:

> Do not be hasty in the laying on of hands, nor take part in the sins of others; keep yourself pure. . . . The sins of some people are conspicuous, going before them to judgment, but the sins of others appear later. So also good works are conspicuous, and even those that are not cannot remain hidden. (1 Tim. 5:22–25)

Encouragement to the Present Pastors

Scripture offers a pattern of life-on-life mentoring—Moses with Joshua, Elijah with Elisha, Jesus with the Twelve, Paul with Timothy. Being kingdom-minded, then, means prioritizing mentorship. One way for us to do this is to make clear pathways for internships, apprenticeships, leadership trainings, and the like.

> "Aspiring overseers must be patient, trusting that the Lord will raise them up to pastor at the right time."

Brother pastor, train your church to see it as her mission, above all other Christian institutions, to prepare men for ministry.[1] Invest your life in fulfilling Paul's exhortation to Timothy: "What you have heard from me in the presence of many witnesses entrust to faithful men, who will be able to teach others also" (2 Tim. 2:2).

Only by immersing aspiring overseers in your life, ministry, and church will you discover who these faithful men are and when they are ready to pastor.

Encouragement to the Aspiring Pastors

Pastoral ministry requires ambition. A man must be driven to serve our King by serving his bride, or he will not last. Ministry is hard, really hard. Spirit-given ambition must be like a "fire in the bones" that pushes one through the discouragements, difficulties, and devastations of pastoral ministry. I have not met many current or aspiring pastors that lack ambition.

Yet let me encourage such men to first direct their ambition towards being trained. Such men must be patient, trusting that the Lord will raise them up to pastor at the right time. Let God's Spirit use God's church and its undershepherds to mold you and tell you when you are ready.

If a man is unwilling to do this, he is not mature enough for the ministry. If his ambition to preach Christ cannot endure training, his ambition will not endure the ministry either.

Aspiring brother, be patient and humble and search for ways to be trained in the local church. Below are some questions you can ask those who will be honest with you in love.

- Do I have the social skills to be able to connect with people?
- How do I handle being told "no" or "not yet"?
- How do I handle conflict?
- Do I humbly receive and extend forgiveness?
- How do I handle being given non-glamorous projects and tasks?
- Do I finish tasks I have been given?
- How do I handle being proven wrong?
- How do I handle having wrong done to me?
- How do I handle that "prickly" church member over time?
- How do I suffer?
- How do I help those who suffer?
- How do I serve the least in the congregation?
- Do I show partiality?
- Am I slow to speak?
- Do I listen to people?
- Do I struggle with the fear of man?
- Am I aware of areas of pride in my life?

The Preacher in Ecclesiastes 7:8 wisely states, "Better is the end of a thing than its beginning, and the patient in spirit is better than the proud in spirit." There is great need for patient preparation. Let us be humble and train well in the beginning, so we can rejoice at the fruit the Lord brings in the end.

---

1. *I would recommend Phil Newton's book* The Mentoring Church *to help teach this.*

Billy Dalton serves as the preaching pastor at First Baptist Church of Cedar Key, Florida.

You Aspire, but Are You Willing?

by Raymond Johnson

Young boys spend their afternoons shooting hoops with hopes of being like Steph Curry. Musicians riff endlessly aspiring to be like The Beatles. Entrepreneurs look for the next big idea like Steve Jobs. Politicians imagine being the next president. Yet as they aspire, they're not always willing to pay the price.

So with young pastors. They dream of preaching like Spurgeon, winning souls like Whitefield, writing theology like Calvin, and pastoring like Baxter. But somewhere along the way their willingness to persist wavers. A congregation opposes them. Their preaching feels futile. The church numbers dwindle. They lose friendships because of a stance they took.

It's easy to aspire to be a great pastor, but are you willing to do all that it takes?

The apostle Peter exhorts pastors to shepherd the flock of God or exercise oversight "not under compulsion, but willingly, as God would have you; not for shameful gain, but eagerly; not domineering over those in your charge, but being examples to the flock" (1 Pet. 5:2–3).

What Shepherds Are Getting Themselves Into

Peter focuses less on what elders should do—"exercising oversight"—and more on *how* they do it. He gives three contrasting pairs of phrases that describe what is appropriate and inappropriate in exercising oversight.

First, shepherds must pastor "not under compulsion, but willingly." They should not just want to *be* shepherds, but *to* shepherd. The impulse to lead must come gladly from within. Otherwise, there is no reason to serve when the demands of or opposition to ministry become heavy.

Second, shepherds must pastor "not for shameful gain, but eagerly." Peter does not mean they should be unpaid. Paul says they should be (cf. 1 Tim. 5:17–18). It's not "gain" that Peter denounces, but "shameful" gain. He doesn't want men who love money, comfort, prestige, platform, and leisure more than the flock of God.

Third, shepherds must not "domineer" but be "examples." Leading, not lording. Any so-called shepherd who is always exerting power, always demanding, always insisting on his own way, always flaunting his position is no willing shepherd of God.

Instead, willing shepherds must be "examples" to the flock. Examples of what? In 1 Peter 2:21–25, he writes,

> For to this you have been called, because Christ also suffered for you, leaving you an example, so that you might follow in his steps. He committed no sin, neither was deceit found in his mouth. When he was reviled, he did not revile in return; when he suffered, he did not threaten, but continued entrusting himself to him who judges justly. He himself bore our sins in his body on the tree, that we might die to sin and live to righteousness. By his wounds you have been healed. For you were straying like sheep, but have now returned to the Shepherd and Overseer of your souls.

A pastor's life should be a picture of the life of Christ for the sheep in "God's flock." He should be an example of humility, self-sacrifice, love for God, passion in congregational worship, generosity, devotion to family, and, most of all, obedience to Jesus in all things. A pastor's life is to match his message, a message he has learned to preach and live by studying the gospel and the life of Jesus Christ.

A Heart Check

So I ask: are you *willing* to pastor?

You may aspire toward pastoring, but are you willing to pastor when friends disassociate themselves from you—or leave the church—because of the counsel you've given?

You want to pastor, but are you willing if the only call to pastor is to a small, rural church in an obscure town?

You may have willingly begun the work of pastoral ministry, but are you willing to continue when the congregation resists your leadership?

You may want to preach and teach, but will you be willing to set aside precious study time to visit a member in the hospital or tend to a broken marriage?

> "You may have willingly begun the work of pastoral ministry, but are you willing to continue when the congregation resists your leadership?"

You may want to begin the work of pastoring as quickly as possible, but are you willing to follow the counsel and leadership of your current pastors, perhaps even to the point of delaying your pursuit of ministry?

You may want to pastor by shepherding others, but are you willing to be shepherded by those currently in authority over you to prepare yourself for the task ahead?

To the aspiring pastor, as you seek to prepare yourself for ministry, seek to grow in your willingness to do the shepherding work that reaps no temporal rewards, but earns an unfading crown of glory.

Recommended Additional Reading

- Bobby Jamieson's *The Path to Being a Pastor: A Guide for the Aspiring* is an excellent resource for those exploring a desire (i.e. aspiration) to serve in pastoral ministry.
- Gregory the Great's *The Book of Pastoral Rule* is helpful in exploring the duties and obligations of pastoral ministry. I suggest this because only reading modern books impoverishes our understanding of pastoral ministry.
- Harold L. Senkbeil's *The Care of Souls: Cultivating A Pastor's Heart* is helpful in highlighting the ordinary tasks of a pastor that are extraordinarily rich in their impact; these ordinary tasks are the heart of the calling of the willing shepherd.
- Eugene Peterson's *The Contemplative Pastor*—despite all my disagreements with Peterson—is helpful because he understood the importance of the minister's pursuit of "congruence": completeness, wholeness, integrity. He understood the gap between our public service and private devotion exposed a problem in our spirituality, even if we "faithfully" prayed regularly, read the Scriptures daily, met in a worshiping local church on Sundays, received baptism, shared in the Lord's Supper, or pastored a congregation.

Raymond Johnson is the senior pastor of Christ Church West Chester in West Chester, Pennsylvania.

Candidate Wisely and Honestly

by Branton Burleson

A pastoral resident of ours recently spoke to another local church's search committee. This congregation is struggling and in dire need of faithful leadership. Surprisingly, this committee member told my friend, "We'll call you back when the weather gets warmer!"

Clearly, this church had lost all sense of urgency in seeking permanent leadership.

Needless to say, candidating can be frustrating and nerve-wracking. If you're wondering what to expect, be encouraged that no single approach exists. Nevertheless, some principles apply to most settings, and the aim of this article is to help aspiring pastors consider how to candidate wisely and honestly with a shepherd-less congregation.

One caveat before I begin: many candidating processes will involve interacting with largely unhealthy churches who have entrusted ill-equipped search teams to recommend the next pastor. That's primarily the context to which I will speak.

1. Research the Church

An aspiring candidate should seek to learn as much as he can about the congregation. Scour the church's website. Talk to the local association and state convention. Ask them what they know about the history of the church. Contact pastors you may be connected to in the area. If it makes sense, ask key people in the community about the church's reputation.

In the initial interview with the search committee, come prepared with thoughtful questions.[1] Seek to understand the congregation's expectations of a pastor. Much like dating, not everything that can be known will be revealed before accepting the call to shepherd a congregation. But the goal prior to accepting the call is to learn the essentials.

2. Know Your Family

The decision to accept a church's call is not the candidate's alone. He should consider the willingness and readiness of his family.

Your wife and children are embarking on this journey with you. What does your wife think? How will this change affect your children? Depending on the demographic of the congregation, your family may be leaving behind many friends. Such changes do not necessarily mean you shouldn't move forward, but it's wise to know how to shepherd your family through these disruptions (1 Tim. 3:4).

It's also important to consider whether the church can meet your family's needs. Be realistic about what your family needs to live in that community. Is this a full-time, bi-vocational, or co-vocational situation? If it isn't full-time, how will this affect the dynamics of your family life, and do you and your wife agree on what that will mean (1 Tim. 5:8)?

3. Know Yourself

When I came to my current congregation, it had been in steep decline for many years. At best, the church had two years of life left. Challenges inside the church and outside in the community were daunting. Ten or fifteen years earlier, I would not have been prepared to lead. So be honest with yourself about your own limitations and readiness. Are you prepared to enter at this point in your congregation's life and lead them to where they need to go?

Additionally, be honest about your own eagerness to serve this particular congregation. Do you genuinely want to pastor there or are you going out of desperation? The qualifications for an elder clearly indicate that overseeing a congregation must be done willingly (1 Tim. 3:1, 1 Pet. 5:2).

4. Don't Mislead, but Don't Sabotage Either

The likelihood of some difficult or complicated questions arising in the process is high. Be prepared to speak to your non-negotiable doctrines. Can you identify them? Can you winsomely articulate your theological distinctives and ministry philosophy? What hills will you die on, and what can you tolerate going in?

Remember, some congregations have so deteriorated in health that they barely can be called churches. But someone must go and lead them back to health again. Expecting too much of the congregation going in will allow discouragement to quickly set in.

Being candid with the search committee early is important to avoid misleading anyone. Be prepared to answer direct questions with honest responses (see 2 Cor. 4:2).

> "Some congregations have so deteriorated in health that they barely can be called churches. But someone must go and lead them back to health again."

At the same time, don't sabotage yourself either. For instance, if a search committee is uninformed about a controversial issue, you'll need to navigate the matter carefully. You want to both be transparent while also not creating fear or controversy where none exists. Some congregations have settled opposition to particular matters, and others don't know that some controversies exist. Assure the search team of your devotion to *the whole counsel of God* (Acts 20:27), and that means you will preach everything that God reveals in his Word, even the complicated and controversial parts.

I recommend requesting a "town hall" style meeting with the congregation before making any final decisions. Before the church I now pastor voted to call me, I met with the whole congregation and fielded their questions. This time allowed me to know what they cared about most and what issues were of greatest concern for them from the start.

5. Lean on Your Sending Church

I'm operating on the assumption that most guys reading this article will be sent from another congregation. If you're not, then I strongly recommend that you consider spending at least a year under the oversight of qualified elders in a healthy congregation.

If this is your situation, then you have the incredible blessing of seeking wisdom in a multitude of godly counselors (Prov. 11:14). Request that your elders assess the prospective congregation with you. Ask them to make you aware of your blind spots, to ask you hard questions, and to tell you hard truths that you need to hear (Prov. 27:6). This is one of the safety nets that Christ has given us in the fellowship of the local church.

6. Trust the Lord

God calls us to walk wisely. Throughout the candidating process, trust him. Remember that God is sovereign and will be with us wherever we go (Heb. 13:5). Settle it in your mind that you won't know everything that you want to know beforehand. And that's okay. You didn't know everything about your wife before you married her. But you knew what you needed to know, and you trusted the Lord with the rest.

When Paul and Barnabas were sent from Antioch, only God knew the challenges they would face. The Holy Spirit told the church to set these men apart, so they fasted and prayed and sent them off (Acts 13:1–2). We have something more certain than exhaustive knowledge about a prospective congregation. We have a sovereign and faithful God who is already there (Matt. 28:20).

---

1. Here are two good sources of questions: Jeff Robinson, "10 Questions Pastoral Candidates Should Ask a Search Team." The Gospel Coalition. January 28, 2020. https://www.thegospelcoalition.org/article/10-questions-pastoral-candidates-should-ask-search-team/. David Prince, "14 Questions to Ask a Pastor Search Committee." Southern Equip. *https://equip.sbts.edu/article/14-questions-to-ask-a-pastor-search-committee/.*

Branton Burleson is the lead pastor of Grace Baptist West Asheville in Asheville, North Carolina.

Section Two

After the Gun: First Five Years

Find a Mentor!

by Cheston Pickard

New pastors find themselves in a variety of situations that yield an exorbitant number of questions.

That's bad news for inexperienced shepherds. But here's some good news: there are pastors who will sit with you, answer questions, and allow you to observe their faith and practice so you won't needlessly stumble in the dark. If you're a new pastor, find one of these pastors! They are vital.

What kind of mentor should you look for? Consider the following.

Find an Exemplary Mentor

When I moved for pastoral training, I began attending a faithful local church that caught my attention with its expositional preaching. I quickly latched on to Pastor Tyler, following him every chance I could get and asking a ton of questions. He was an exemplary model in two ways.

First, he followed Jesus with a holy consistency. The Tyler behind the pulpit was the same man you would find in the coffee shop, at the service planning meetings, and at home with his wife and kids. Second, Pastor Tyler lived with a holy intentionality—with chapter and verse attached to everything he did. He wanted his life to point to God's Word, desiring that people would know and follow Jesus.

Pastor Tyler was "exemplary," but he was not "flawless." All men are sinners, and the closer you get to a man, the more you will see his blemishes. But don't let that deter you. Find a man who seeks to be faithful to Christ, faithful to Scripture, and faithful to the qualifications of his office.

Find an Experienced Mentor

In any line of work, it is wise to listen to men who have "been there and done that." For me, there was nothing quite like the car rides, coffees, and table talks with Brother Jimmy, a pastor for over thirty years. I would pick his brain whenever I got the chance. He was familiar with nearly every situation I would bring to the table.

Among all of Brother Jimmy's incredible counsel, two lessons stand out. First, ministry is not about starting well, but finishing well. If you're in ministry long enough, sadly, plenty of men around you will fall because they failed to watch over their life and doctrine.

Second, we can learn from both the positive and negative experience of others. Just like the man who passed along the sluggard's house, we can look and receive instruction (Prov. 24:30–32). Those who have shipwrecked their ministry, their marriages, or even their faith teach us to guard our hearts from going down the same destructive paths.

I'm grateful to have found a joyful soldier to lead me down faithful paths.

Find an Eager Mentor

Mentoring is relational. Don't pursue a mentor unless they are eager to prioritize their time with you, and vice versa. A short-lived mentorship won't bear much fruit.

When I finished seminary, I immediately entered the pastorate at a rural church and just as quickly needed a few pointers. I took a leap of faith and sent an email to Pastor Brian, asking him if he would spend time with me. He didn't know me well but answered, "Yes! Let's get coffee next week and chat!" Pastor Brian proceeded to meet with me weekly for six months and let me ask him questions, such as:

- What book of the Bible do I preach first?
- What should hospital visits look like?
- How do I balance my week between church and family?
- How do you preside over a business meeting?
- How do you preach a funeral for an unbeliever?

Pastor Brian was eager and gracious to spend time with me, and he prioritized his investment. A few minutes each week made an enormous impact on my life and ministry.

Find an Encouraging Mentor

On this side of heaven, there will be seasons when complaints come in herds, when change is contentious, when relationships are strained (perhaps even your own marriage), when leadership is exhausting, when giving is down, when more people seem to leave your church than join, and when there aren't many wins to celebrate. Sometimes, ministry can feel like a derailed train; anything and everything is keeping your flock from moving in a biblical direction.

The grind of ministry can take a toll on a pastor's mind and heart. Many days downheartedness and disappointment get the best of those in ministry. Satan loves to discourage. That's why pastors need mentors who are great encouragers, those who lead brothers to get up off the floor, pick up their swords, and press on.

Find an Edifying Mentor

Mentoring is discipling. Remember Pastor Tyler? Even though I always called him that out of respect, my wife and I were hesitant about joining his local church, only because we were ignorant about the importance of church membership.

One day, Pastor Tyler nailed me with an ecclesiological truth bomb. "I love that you are benefitting from the sermons, and I'm glad to have you guys around. You're always welcome at the church. But here's the thing: if you're not a member of the flock entrusted to me, then I'm not your pastor."

I left that meeting irritated. *Who cares about membership?* I thought. *Does it really matter as long as I show up and drop some cash in the offering plate?*

After a couple days, I cooled down and asked him to elaborate. First, Pastor Tyler established Scripture's authority. God gets the last word. Second, he led me to recognize Christ's headship, pointing me to Matthew 16:18 to show that local churches belong to Jesus. Christ is the chief. Lastly, Pastor Tyler demonstrated the heart of pastoral ministry. At its most basic level, the pastor's job description is to point the flock to the person and work of Jesus Christ by opening, explaining, and applying God's Word (1 Pet. 5:1–4). And who is his flock? Look at the membership!

Pastor Tyler's mentorship led me to change direction and take part in God's program—the local church. His words stung a little, but faithful are the wounds of a friend (Prov. 27:6). That single conversation changed my life and prepared me for future leadership.

Conclusion

So, find a mentor—for your sake, for your family's sake, for your people's sake, and for Christ's sake. With the technology available today, there is no reason you can't find a mentor, join a cohort, or meet with brothers who have walked down the roads that await you.

Cheston Pickard is a discipleship pastor of Highview Baptist Church in Louisville, Kentucky.

Be a Strong and Courageous Young Leader

by Clint Darst

At some point, every pastor discovers that pastoring is more complex than he anticipated.

You need more strength and courage to lead than you imagined. Like Paul, you ask, "Who is sufficient for these things?" (2 Cor. 2:16).

Brother pastor, where will you turn for strength and courage in those moments?

Lean into God's Presence

First, since insecurity and fearfulness always lurk, remember that God has not only called you, he's promised to be with you.

Moses, overwhelmed with his calling, asked, "Who am I that I should go to Pharaoh and bring the children of Israel out of Egypt?" Yahweh corrected him, "But I will be with you" (Exod. 3:11–12). Joshua succeeded Moses and was given the same promise from the Lord, "Just as I was with

Moses, so I will be with you. I will not leave you or forsake you" (Josh. 1:5). King David passed his mantle to Solomon saying, "Be strong and courageous and do it. Do not be afraid and do not be dismayed, for the Lord God, even my God, is with you. He will not leave you or forsake you, until all the work for the service of the house of the Lord is finished" (1 Chr. 28:20). Christ, our Lord, commissioned us to make disciples and promised to be with us until the end of the age (Matt. 28:19–20). The apostle Paul reminded young Timothy to guard the good deposit entrusted to him by the Holy Spirit who dwells *within* (2 Tim. 1:14).

Brother pastor, where will you find strength and courage to lead when an influential leader or member whom you believed was in your corner suddenly turns on you? Where will you turn when your suggestion of a budget cut to what seems like an obviously unnecessary line item explodes a relational land mine? What will keep your heart at peace when, after teaching on a particular sin, a long-time member who has lived unconfronted in that sin for years wants to meet with you?

In these moments, remember that the same God who called and promised to be with Moses, Joshua, David, Solomon, Paul, and Timothy is present with you. He even dwells within you. You are never alone in this labor. Your weaknesses and limitations are no threat to God's ability to accomplish his purposes. In those moments that require great courage and strength, the same God who rescued Israel from Egypt is with you.

> "Your weaknesses and limitations are no threat to God's ability to accomplish his purposes."

Lean into his presence. Run to him in private prayer and plead that he would empower you for your task.

Lead with God's Word

Second, young pastors in need of strength and courage must remember that God's Word is living and active and will accomplish all that he wills in the life of the church (Heb. 4:12, Isa. 55:10–11).

In addition to reminding Joshua of his presence, God commanded his servant to be "strong and very courageous, being careful to do according to all the law that Moses my servant commanded you. Do not turn from it to the right hand or to the left, that you may have good success wherever you go" (Josh. 1:7). Similarly, when Jeremiah brings his insecurity to the Lord, saying, "Ah, Lord God! Behold, I do not know how to speak, for I am only a youth," the Lord instructs, "Do not say, 'I am only a youth'; for to all to whom I send you, you shall go, and *whatever I command you,* you shall speak. Do not be afraid of them, for I am with you to deliver you, declares the Lord" (Jer. 1:7–8). Or consider the source of Paul's lion-like courage as he writes from a cold dark prison to his young protégé in the faith, "I am suffering, bound with chains as a criminal. But the Word of God is not bound!" (2 Tim. 2:9).

Young pastor, when a congregation looks to you for leadership, but you also sense them looking *at* you to determine if they are willing to follow your leadership, lead with the Word. Let them see that your goal is not to get them to follow you as an end but to help them follow Christ in his Word.

And do this with great humility, especially as a young pastor. Embrace life in the fishbowl. Let them observe you submitted to the Word by sharing what you are personally convicted, instructed, and encouraged by. As Paul exhorted young Timothy, let them see your progress (1 Tim. 4:11–13). And make sure there is consistency between your public and private ministry of the Word. Don't be as bold as a lion in the pulpit but as cowardly as a house cat in private. Be a humble beast in both. If you rightly handle the Word of truth in both places, then you will have the clear conscious necessary to lead with courage and strength (Acts 20:20, 2 Tim. 2:15).

In those moments you're tempted to run and hide, do so behind the text of Scripture. Lead your congregation with the bold humility that comes from a personal submission to the Word and a right fear of the Lord that is genuinely concerned not with pleasing man, but with pleasing Christ (Gal. 1:10).

Brother pastor, maybe you are still in the honeymoon phase of your pastorate. Maybe things are running smoothly. Praise God for that! But eventually, this calling will demand more strength and courage than you might now imagine. When that day comes and you ask with the war-torn apostle, "Who is sufficient for these things?" remember his answer, "Our sufficiency is from God" (2 Cor. 3:5).

God is with you, pastor, and he has spoken. Lean into his presence, and lead with his Word. Be strong and courageous.

Clint Darst is the lead pastor of King's Cross Church in Greensboro, North Carolina.

Patience! Pick Your Battles Wisely

by Jeramie Rinne

"**P**ick your battles." This phrase is commonly given to new pastors because there are battles aplenty to be fought.

Young pastor, as you settle into the ministry, you will likely identify an array of things you desire to change, from the weighty to the trivial: changing bylaws, updating the sanctuary lighting, hiring (or firing) a staff member, reviewing the membership rolls, reformatting the bulletin, introducing new songs, repainting the offices, overhauling the children's curriculum. What a list!

Common sense tells you that you can't address all those issues immediately. You lack the time, expertise, institutional knowledge, and, perhaps most importantly, the relational capital to tackle everything everywhere all at once. Generals avoid wars on multiple fronts, and wise pastors should know how to pick their battles carefully.

But which battles should you pick? How do you prioritize change? Why should you renovate this but wait on that? These are questions I'm currently wrestling through. Though I have been a senior pastor for over 26 years, I'm now in my third congregation, and I'm in yet another initial five-year window. In all three churches, I've learned that wisely picking battles depends on many factors. An easy win for a pastor in Church A might be a suicide mission for a pastor in Church B. That said, here are five categories of issues you might consider prioritizing earlier on in your ministry.

1. Pre-Loaded Issues

Pick battles that have been declared prior to your first day on the job. Sometimes, the church declares the battle. At my second pastorate, the governing board told me up front they wanted to transition to an elder model. When I arrived, we immediately went to work and amended the bylaws in less than a year and a half.

Sometimes the pastor declares the battle before arriving. At my current church, I made it clear on the front end that, if they called me, I would lead them to replace their council and committees with biblical elders and deacons. We amended our bylaws after three years.

In fact, I strongly encourage pastors to put major, foreseeable changes on the table during the candidating process. As I've heard another pastor say, "Try to get fired during the interview." Declaring your intentions up front is a kindness to the church and a safeguard for you. When the church picks you, they're also picking the battles you declared. This principle doesn't guarantee a problem-free process, but it does give you a mandate of sorts and sets a priority for you.

2. Biblical Church Patterns

Speaking of elders and deacons . . . choose to pursue the Bible's priorities and patterns for the church. Here I'm thinking of structural things: church membership, Bible-saturated and Bible-governed corporate worship, the right administration of the ordinances, and the congregation exercising the "keys of the kingdom" (Matt. 16:19, cf. 18:18) both in joining members and removing members. All of this requires clarity on the offices of elder and deacon.

But that's not all. Prioritize expository preaching, evangelism, disciple-making, praying for and modeling a one-another culture of mutual edification, and church planting. All these disciplines help the church's gospel work. The church is Jesus's, so when he speaks about his church's form and function, we need to prioritize and apply what he says.

Of course, picking these battles doesn't mean trying to win them in a day, or even a year. It takes time to teach a church what Scripture says. It takes even more time to persuade your people that biblical patterns bring greater blessings than mere tradition. Furthermore, implementation often progresses slowly and in stages. When it comes to these changes, remember the adage *festina lente*: "make haste slowly."

Here's the point: aim for biblical priorities regardless of how long it takes. Don't let the skirmishes of daily ministry distract you from your focus on the long-term, strategic campaign of teaching your people to obey everything Jesus has commanded in his Word.

3. Crises of Gospel Integrity

Sometimes you don't pick your battles. They erupt around you. In these moments, you must fight for the sake of the church and the integrity of its gospel witness. Suppose you discover in the first few months that the deacon chair has been having an affair with the associate pastor's wife; or that the office administrator—who happens to be the daughter of a prominent family—has been embezzling; or that an influential adult Sunday school teacher has been teaching the prosperity gospel.

It's extremely risky for you, as a new pastor, to hit these crises head-on. It could cost you your job. But these sorts of situations are so egregious that you have no choice but to run toward the fire. The honor of Jesus's name placed on your church is at stake. You didn't pick these battles, but God has sovereignly picked them for you, and you must stand for his glory.

4. Providential Opportunities

Other times, you pick a battle not because it's so calamitous but because it's so easy. In fact, there's no real battle at all. God moves mysteriously and an opportunity for progress arises. Grab it! Be opportunistic, in the best sense of that term. In my experience, church reform progresses through intentional, slow leadership as well as through non-linear, surprising providences.

I came to my current church during COVID. Like congregations around the world, our church had implemented a livestream option. I'm opposed to livestream (i.e., viewing the service online, on Sunday morning, in real time) because it tempts people to forsake the assembly and causes them to think about Jesus's church in consumeristic ways. How exactly does one "attend online"?

Then an opportunity came. A monster hurricane wiped out our church building. We had to meet in another church's facility for months where we didn't have livestream capability. I took advantage of that strange providence and never restarted the livestream. We reverted to the old-fashioned method of recording the sermon and posting it later in the week.

Be on the lookout for such low-hanging fruit. You will often find that God already prepared the soil for you. He may have even provided the people around you to help get it done. I've often seen how the Lord has raised up pivotal influencers within the church's leadership and membership. Trust their local knowledge for how and when to move forward.

5. The Fiercest Battle of All

There's one more battle that you must pick. It's a fight that will dramatically affect the future of you and your church. And it's the fiercest fight of all.

Brother pastor, you must fight impatience in your own heart.

Yes, there are battles to pick early on. But more often than not, you will serve your church better by being patient, slowing down, and playing the long game. The list of battles not to pick is much longer than you think.

> "It takes time to persuade your people that biblical patterns bring greater blessings than mere tradition."

How do you fight impatience? Fight it with faith in God's Word. Trust that God will work in the hearts of his people through faithful expository preaching applied to the life of the church. Help your people see, week after week, how God's Word not only speaks to their personal lives but also to the church's corporate life. Then trust the Holy Spirit to work in his time. The most helpful thing you can do for your church as a new pastor is establish the pulpit with faithful, gospel-centered exposition. Could it be that our impatience with the church reveals our lack of confidence in the sufficiency and power of Scripture?

Resist impatience with prayer. Make a list of all the things you wish you could change at your church. Then commit them to prayer and wait on the Lord. You will be amazed at how God answers prayers in the most surprising ways.

Battle impatience with humility. What if some of the problems or flaws you see in the church are matters of indifference, or even strengths? What if things you want to change are merely reflective of your own personal preferences, culture, or conscience? Could your impatience be borne of personal insecurities or pride? Cultivate the grace of self-suspicion.

Finally, kill impatience with love. Your church is not fundamentally an organization to be restructured, a problem to be solved, or an ideal to be realized. It's an assembly of the blood-bought children of God. Your church is Jesus's household, Jesus's bride, Jesus's flock. Impatient pastors often love the idea of the church more than the people in the church. But Jesus loves them. And he's slowly, patiently, and gently maturing his children, preparing his bride, and leading his flock.

May Jesus fill us, his undershepherds and stewards, with his love and patience for his saints.

Jeramie Rinne is an author and the senior pastor of Sanibel Community Church in Sanibel, Florida.

Loving Your Family While Leading God's Church

by Liam Garvie

I've been a pastor for nineteen years. Looking back on my first five years makes me want to buy a time-traveling DeLorean (remember *Back to the Future?*) or phone booth (remember *Bill and Ted's Excellent Adventure?*), so that I could go back and advise my younger self. Too many Saturday nights were spent in the study upstairs while my wife sat alone downstairs watching television. Too many opportunities to be a godly example to the church family that I loved were missed precisely because I didn't love my family first.

As a 25-year-old starting out, 1 Timothy 4:12 was my favorite verse to rehearse. I wanted to be an example so that no one despised me for my youth. Yet the example I set in those first five years threatened something worse than church members despising my youth; it threatened to hinder their own godliness. The two, after all, are linked.

If I could go back in time, I'd tell 25-year-old me to re-read his favorite "verse to rehearse" and say, set a good example for the church by being a godly man in the home *first*. How does one set such an example?

1. Through Exemplary Speaking

Youthful fervor in ministry can hinder good communication in the home. Is that your experience? Too often I had to be finger-snapped out of ministry daydreams. Some exegetical question or pastoral predicament clogged up my brain. I was there, but I wasn't there. Worse, when the pitter-patter of tiny wee feet brought with it a tiny wee knock at the study door, the sense of inconvenience led to intemperate speech that neither built up nor tasted of grace. So sad.

Yet exemplary speaking means *actually* speaking with your wife and kids. It means being interested and undistracted as you discover all that's going on in their lives. In a word, engage! And watch your tongue. It's a fire, and irritation-sparked house fires can render useless your ministerial fervor. So take care to practice exemplary speaking where it matters most.

2. Through Exemplary Conduct

I remember those early days of ministry when I was desperate for a church whose life and conduct marked it off from its community. But too often in my first five years, home life looked different than the Christian life I exhorted others to live. When conduct in the home lags behind the conduct we commend, we're falling into hypocrisy. Our homes ought to be showrooms for gospel living in a natural environment. We should be more concerned to live rightly in front of our family than our flock. If we can't care for our house, then how can we care for God's?

3. Through Exemplary Love

A pastor's first foray into service is fueled by books that compel us toward a love-driven ministry. These are the blood-bought people of God. Our love for them should reflect Christ's love for them, and his love led to laying down his life. But I remember many occasions in those opening phases of ministry when I sacrificed more to serve the ministry than I did to serve my family. What a terrible example to set. The church was going through a hard time, a healing time. But that was no excuse.

If Bill and Ted's phone booth landed in front of 25-year-old me, I'd jump out and say, "Reorder those priorities, ya dafty!" Better to preach a nearly finished sermon or postpone a meeting than to sacrifice time with your wife and family. What a difference it will make to your church family for them to see you love your wife deeply from the heart (1 Pet. 1:22), the kind of love that commends Christ to all (John 13:35)?

4. Through Exemplary Faith

Pastors who want their church to live by faith in all that God has said should scan their home life for proof that they themselves do. That trust will certainly be tested in the first five years! Some of my most difficult experiences of church leadership came in that period. There were factions, accusations, ultimatums. Ugly stuff, really. Personal challenges came thick and fast in those times (I'll spare you the details). Immaturity and impatience led too quickly to doubt and despair, not in front of members, but in front of my wife and kids.

Time-traveling me would tell the younger version, "Trust in the Lord with all your heart" (Prov. 3:5). God's grace is sufficient for every trial (2 Cor. 12:9), and his sovereignty a soft pillow on which to lay your head. Take God at his infallible Word, and always live like it's true. Let your family learn that first through the example of your faith, a faith that steadies theirs.

5. Through Exemplary Purity

In many cases, when being in your first five years means being young, then the passions of youth that Paul warns of have likely been fled only recently or, indeed, remain a present threat (2 Tim. 2:22). The most prevalent threat to the purity of young men, it seems, is pornography. Sins like these practiced in secret create a barrier in one's affections and a fog of shame at home. But it's far from being the only

> "We should be more concerned to live rightly in front of our family than our flock."

threat. Purity is holiness, and holiness is hindered if we fail to pull up weeds of sin and plant flowers of virtue.

So, if gray-haired me turned up at the door of brown-haired me, I'd appeal for him not to underestimate how important holiness at home is for the church. I'd warn him against allowing the home to be the place where his guard is let down.

A Good Example in the Church

Listen, being a godly man in the home is vital to being a good example in the church. And being a good example in the church is crucial to the church's health. That's true whether you are in your first five years or your last. Indeed, writing this article is a timely refresher for me.

But in that initial phase, while you're finding your ministry legs, pay special attention to setting an example for the believers in speech, in conduct, in love, in faith, and in purity (1 Tim. 4:12).

Liam Garvie is the associate pastor of Charlotte Chapel in Edinburgh, Scotland.

Take Heart: Preaching to Encourage

by Tiago Oliveira

Young pastor, as you step into your role as shepherd, consider these three important exhortations concerning how to preach sermons that encourage the flock God has entrusted to you.

1. Preach the Word, Not Your Wisdom

"I charge you in the presence of God and of Christ Jesus . . . Preach the word." (2 Tim. 4:1–2)

Pastors have a primary and simple task: preach the Word! This means that preaching should normally consist of reading, explaining, and applying the Word of God to our church and its members. This kind of preaching is often referred to as "expositional" because it exposes God's Word to God's people. The Scriptures alone, under the illumination of the Spirit, bring new life. The Word is not a mere collection of ancient texts from which we simply gain moral instruction or self-help tips. Rather, the Word of God is living and active (Heb. 4:12). God's Word is powerful enough to bring dry bones to life (Ezek. 37:1–14).

Our goal in preaching, therefore, is to help our people deepen their trust in God and his Word, not to garner admiration or allegiance for ourselves. Remember that you are the messenger, not the message! Preach the Bible (and the Bible alone) so that you might lead the church to trust the one who is trustworthy. As you focus on preaching the Word of God, the church will be encouraged and grounded in the truth.

2. Trust the Spirit, Not Your Eloquence

"The wind blows where it wishes, and you hear its sound, but you do not know where it comes from or where it goes. So it is with everyone who is born of the Spirit." (John 3:8)

Young pastor, your success in pastoral ministry does not rest in your natural ability to convince and change people. Instead, you succeed and people are changed when you trust the Holy Spirit's power to use the preached Word for his purposes. The pastor's duty is to preach, not perform. We should want our preaching to persuade (2 Cor. 5:11), but only while acknowledging that the convincing power belongs to the Holy Spirit. Convicting hearts is the Holy Spirit's job (John 16:8), and he works according to God's mysterious and sovereign will (John 3:8).

When we stop relying on our eloquence, creativity, or charisma, we acknowledge our role as instruments through which the Holy Spirit works. This frees us from the pressure of results-oriented preaching and allows us to trust the Spirit's transformative power. As the apostle Paul stated, "My speech and my message were not in plausible words of wisdom, but in demonstration of the Spirit and of power, so that your faith might not rest in the wisdom of men but in the power of God" (1 Cor. 2:4–5).

3. Show Them Christ, Not You!

"For what we proclaim is not ourselves, but Jesus Christ as Lord, with ourselves as your servants for Jesus's sake." (2 Cor. 4:5)

Finally, the heart of a sermon should always be Christ and his gospel. The pastor is not the church's savior, Jesus is! What people need is to meet the living God in the person of Christ. He is the one they should fully trust. Therefore, your commitment should mirror Paul's: "For I decided to know nothing among you except Jesus Christ and him crucified" (1 Cor. 2:2). Show them the Son and his finished work, and it will be enough.

In every sermon, we should point the church to Jesus, our Savior and our Lord. Our identity as Christ's servants is not to draw attention to ourselves but to lead people to the Lord Jesus (2 Cor. 4:5). Young pastor, be happy to be left out of the picture when your members reflect on last Sunday's sermon. To preach encouraging sermons, Christ must increase and you must decrease.

Conclusion

As you step into your new church, you are called not only to lead but also to encourage. Proper encouragement, as understood through the Scripture, is found in pointing people to Christ. As you have been entrusted to care for the sheep in your church, strive to center your ministry on preaching the Word, trusting the Holy Spirit, and showing them Christ and his gospel.

Tiago Oliveira serves as the senior pastor at First Baptist Church of Lisbon and leads Martin Bucer Seminary Portugal.

Young Pastor, Care for the Older Members of Your Flock

by Dave Kiehn

B. F. Hawkins pastored Park Baptist Church from 1944–1958. Under Hawkins's ministry, Park grew to over 500 people in Sunday School and 600 in weekly worship. He led the church to build the facility on Main Street, where it has stood since 1951.

When I became the pastor of Park Baptist Church in 2012, more than half of the membership had come to Christ under his ministry. The man was a spiritual giant. I prayed often in those early years that my ministry would bear similar spiritual fruit.

Shortly into my tenure at Park Baptist, however, the challenge was clear: our older members longed for church like it was under B. F. Hawkins. I began to pray, "Lord, help our senior saints believe that the best days of Park Baptist Church are ahead of her and not behind her." I wanted them to believe that God was not done with our church.

In those early years of ministry, I focused on shepherding faithful older members. I both failed and succeeded. Below are some lessons I learned along the way. May the Lord use these encouragements and admonitions to help you shepherd the flock of God that is among you.

Preach Christ-Centered Expositional Sermons

When I came to Park Baptist, my congregation had been starved of faithful preaching for about twenty years. It's not that the Word was never preached—it was. But it was rarely preached expositionally.

Senior saints need what every member needs. They need to see Jesus Christ in all the Scriptures. They need to be taught the Word of God.

The best thing I did to pastor these older saints was to preach the Word week after week. So many would stop me at the door after service and thank me for holding out the Bible to them.

Part of caring for elderly sheep means feeding the starved soul.

Love Your People

In church revitalization, senior saints are sometimes characterized as burdens for the pastor. They're the ones you have to deal with before all the young people will supposedly start coming to the church. But Jesus loves these older saints—and because he loves them, you as their pastor should love them too.

Love them from your heart. They're a blessing, not a burden.

As I reflect on those early years, I recall taking some of my senior members to the apple orchard with my toddlers, sitting on picnic tables eating apple cider donuts, and talking about their late husbands. These are some of my fondest memories.

Spend Time in Prayer and the Word Together

Seniors love to be visited by their pastors. As life slows down, time becomes increasingly precious. How encouraging that they want to spend some of that time with you, their pastor. What a privilege!

Pastor, spend time in prayer and the Word with your older members. Go to their house, open your Bible, and talk through your recent sermon points. Ask them what they're reading in the Word.

During the early years at our church, I spent every other Tuesday morning studying the Bible and praying with older saints. We would pray for wayward children and grandchildren. We would talk about how God was moving in the church. I would invite them to pray for me and the church's ministry.

Spending time is important, but spending time around God's Word is especially valuable to them and to you.

Learn Their Stories and the Church's Story

The Bible calls gray hair "a crown of glory" (Prov. 16:31). This is because, in part, longer life often means more wisdom.

So listen and ask questions of older members. Learn their stories. Empathize with their pain. Rejoice with their triumphs.

As you learn their story, ask them about your church's story too. Discover the seasons of pain and the times of growth. This may help you understand why they disagree with you or are fearful of your strategies.

By the time I showed up, our deacons had been holding the church together for twenty years under rocky pastoral leadership. Knowing their troubles and sacrifice helped me understand why it was hard for them to follow my leadership. When we know our people, we can better understand and serve them.

Remind Them of Their Value

Every member is called to use their gifts to build up the body of Christ. As members age, they will slow down. When that happens, they'll be tempted to equate their lack of capacity with a diminished value in the church.

Pastor, help your senior saints resist this mindset. Encourage them to use all their station in life for the glory of God. Remind them how valuable their prayers are. Remind them of the power of a warm smile and a kind word.

Our church grew in part because of the welcoming spirit so many of our senior saints displayed as college students and young families entered our sanctuary.

Prepare Them to Meet Jesus

Pastor, don't wait to visit your people. As I write this, my eyes fill with tears as I think of those I put off visiting and missed praying for before they went to glory. When the Holy Spirit pricks your heart, leave the study, go to the nursing home or wherever your seniors are, and lay hands on those who are nearing their departure. Our job is to help our people get safely to Jesus. This, in part, means shepherding them to the very end.

Max Phillips joined Park Baptist Church when he was fourteen years old. He remained a member of the church until he died at 99. We had breakfast together once a month for ten years. He wasn't afraid to tell me things he didn't like about what I was doing, but I knew he loved me. When he died, it hit me harder than I expected. He was 99. It was supposed to happen. I knew it was coming, but I still wasn't ready. I realized that in God's kindness, Max had become one of my closest friends. As I tried to minister to his soul, he cared for mine. I still miss him.

Max came to Christ under B. F. Hawkins's preaching and served the church faithfully for years. One Sunday, Max stopped me at the door, looked me dead in the eyes, and said, "Preacher, our church is more alive today than it's ever been." My prayers were answered. The longer I pastor, the more I cherish those saints.

Dave Kiehn is the senior pastor of the Park Baptist Church in Rock Hill, South Carolina.

Make the Main Thing the Main Thing on Sundays

by Bret Capranica

I f everything in a church needs to change, where should a pastor start? I want to offer a convictional testimony for making the Bible the main course on Sunday. Every other change should follow.

When I arrived at my church, it had a solid theological foundation, a history of expository preaching, and a membership that was eager to serve. Still, it was awash with so much transition that every ministry was crying for attention. As the new pastor, the situation felt overwhelming. But I was convinced that the table we set on Sunday would determine the whole ministry, and our main course had to be the Word of God.

Preach the Word

What a preacher does on Sunday with the Bible will determine how the rest of the church will treat the Bible. Thin sermons, thin church. Robust sermons, robust church. Therefore, if I don't shape my week around study and preparation, I will be dominated by other urgencies, leading to inconsistent and insignificant exposition.

Prioritizing Sunday's exposition has been the catalyst of comprehensive change. A growing disparity between how the Word was handled in the sermon and how it was handled in other areas of ministry became evident. As the Word changed people, their expectations and approach to ministry changed. Making expository preaching the main course every Sunday influenced every other side dish on our congregational table.

Sing the Word

When the Word of Christ dominates God's people, they begin to sing the themes of Scripture to one another before the Lord (Col. 3:16). When I arrived, I did not find the lyrics of our songs to be unbiblical, but we sang so many songs each year that their biblical content could not "richly dwell within us." Further, our musicians did not share a common view of Scripture, the local church, or the purpose of congregational singing. As a disparity began to grow between how the Bible was handled in the sermon and how the Bible was sung on Sunday, the expectation of those being shaped by the Word changed.

In my first year, I taught through Revelation 4 and 5, showing what heavenly worship emphasized and asking us to consider how heaven's worship might impact ours. Those sermons became foundational for material and conversations that led us to reexamine what we sang, how we sang, who should lead our singing, and how we would emphasize the congregation singing.

> "What a preacher does on Sunday with the Bible will determine how the rest of the church will treat the Bible."

Today, an elder oversees a biblically faithful and congregationally committed group of musicians. They all possess a serious approach to Scripture and devotion to the local church and our singing together.

Singing the Word on Sunday has spread to other ministries, too—like families at home and small groups before they discuss sermon application. We have even sung Sunday's songs at the bedside of a dying member. A Word-dominated Sunday shapes lives well beyond it.

Pray the Word

Preaching and singing the Word also made the elders reconsider the centrality of Scripture in corporate prayer. We studied how Scripture calls the church to pray and produced a guide for the elders to use in their public prayers. This provided members a model of how to pray throughout the week.

Every aspect of our Sunday morning gathering is connected to Scripture and prayer. A psalm calls us to worship, and we respond to its content in prayer. An elder uses a specific passage to shape his intercessions. The sermon text is read, followed by a plea for God to give us collective understanding.

The sermon is preached, and we ask for grace to apply it.

Our Sunday evening gathering is designed around Jesus's instruction in Matthew 6:9–13, with emphases of adoration, intercession, confession, and submission, each connected to a passage of Scripture that guides how we pray. As we have prioritized praying biblically on Sunday, we have witnessed our members prioritizing prayer in their small groups and as they disciple one another.

Display the People of the Word

Paul describes baptism as our immersion by the Spirit into the body of Christ, made visible through our immersion by water into the local church (1 Cor. 12:13). He also describes the Lord's Supper as a corporate sign of the body of Christ as we partake of the bread and cup together (1 Cor. 10:16–17). Yes, the ordinances require a personal faith to participate, but they declare who the corporate people of faith are.

In my first year, we observed the Lord's Supper only three times, with more emphasis on an elaborate distribution of the elements than their meaning. In most minds, baptism was disassociated from church membership and was offered to some who could provide little credible evidence of conversion. Some thought requiring baptism before participating in the Lord's Supper was a strange new doctrine I had deceptively introduced, though it had been explicit in our doctrinal statement from the church's beginning.

That year, I intentionally preached passages on the corporate aspects of baptism and the Lord's Supper. We changed the frequency of observing the Lord's Supper (to at least monthly) and lingered longer in how we participated. I also started to ask those being baptized to publicly share evidence of their conversion.

Members are now eager to invite non-Christians to attend when we baptize, and the congregation is exuberant when a new Christian is connected to the body in baptism. We underestimate how the ordinances enhance the witness of the church and display the people of the Word.

Make the Word the Main Course

Making the Word the main course on Sunday has transformed everything in our church. The transformation among us is not a result of our own ingenuity or creativity. The Word has done the work.

Bret Capranica is a pastor-teacher of Summit Woods Baptist Church in Lee's Summit, Missouri.

Creating Healthy Membership Practices

by Jon Deedrick

It's day one of your new pastorate. You've inherited a church with meaningless membership.[1] What in the world are you to do? What membership practices should you implement?

As a new pastor, there's a type of triage required of you. Not a triage of what's urgent (like the triage unit at your local emergency room), but a triage of what's wise. There are things you should do *immediately* and things you should do *eventually*. It's your job to triage toward that end.

Let me give you an idea of how this might look.

Things to Do Immediately

1. Make Corporate Applications in Your Sermons

As you give yourself to Christ-centered expositional preaching, help your people connect the dots between the gospel and its implications for the corporate life of the church. Point them frequently from the text to the "why" of your church's philosophy of ministry. If the Lord produces change in your church, it won't be through the force of your personality; only the Spirit of God through the Word of God produces lasting change.

2. Pray Publicly about Healthy Membership Practices

Praying publicly for your church's body life sets a tone of priorities. Utilize your pastoral prayer. The congregation will learn what you and the elders value.

For instance, you might pray that the Lord would grant your church a warm culture of discipling and evangelism, an atmosphere where it's natural for your members to work for the spiritual good of others. You could pray for transparent relationships to flourish among your congregation. Toward the top of the prayer list should always be humility and gospel unity.

One caveat: be careful not to passive-aggressively "subtweet" the church or individual members when you pray. One of the worst things you could do is try to shame your members into action. Rather, hold out a cheerful vision of how you hope the church will look one day.

3. Teach about the Local Church

I don't think it's hyperbole to say that most Christians today think the local church is less important than God does. If your membership practices are flimsy, I guarantee your people's understanding of what a church is and does is poor.

There are multiple ways to equip your people with biblical ecclesiology.

> "As a new pastor, there's a type of triage required of you. Not a triage of what's urgent (like the triage unit at your local emergency room), but a triage of what's wise."

- Include the doctrine of the church in your rotation of discipleship classes or offer it as a modular class for those who want more than your regular curriculum.
- Preach through an epistle like Ephesians or 1 Timothy that puts strong ecclesiological pillars in place.
- Preach a topical series on a church's practices[2] or the corporate implications of the ordinances.

4. Start a Regular Prayer Meeting

Nothing unifies a church like praying together. Through prayer, God works and love grows.

A pragmatic benefit of prayer meetings is that you'll quickly discover who the committed and growing members are, a core that will hopefully grow over time. I'd encourage you to make your prayer meetings highly relational and focus on the church's mission of making disciples. In addition to soliciting requests from the congregation, have a set of standing requests[3] with a Great Commission heartbeat.

5. Distribute a Membership Directory

A wise man once called a church's membership directory "a Christian's second most important book."[4] A published directory not only raises the visibility profile of your membership, but it also becomes a tool to increase connectivity and prayer. Encourage your congregation to pray for a handful of members each day. Even if they don't yet understand the "why" of meaningful membership, they'll start to intuitively sense its importance.

Of course, this idea isn't any good unless you refresh the directory whenever you welcome new members. A printed directory is the most age-inclusive format, but plenty of church software apps make a digital directory available for tech-savvy members.

6. Hold a Membership Class

You might be tempted to wait on this one, but I wouldn't recommend it.[5] A required class for prospective members helps instill your desired DNA in all newcomers, and it implicitly signals the importance of membership to the entire congregation.

This class should teach what the church expects of its members and what the members can expect from the church. A good place to start is your church's statement of faith, covenant, and history.

7. Interview Prospective Members

If someone completes the class and wants to move forward in membership, have one of the elders interview the candidate about his testimony and understanding of the gospel. It's shocking how much pastoral work gets done in these conversations—from discerning false professions, to diagnosing the need for baptism, to discovering sin struggles. Take these times seriously; they're an essential way that elders protect and foster regenerate church membership.

This conversation also provides a natural time to reiterate the expectations and commitments of becoming part of your church family.

8. Model Meaningful Membership

One of the most important things you do in any season of pastoral ministry is model what you teach. Concerning membership, work hard early to develop relationships. Invite members to your home. Disciple them. Encourage them. Care for them. Be honest with them. Let them know that you're a church member first and pastor second.

If you practice what you preach, in time you may look over your shoulder and see many others imitating you.

Things to Do Eventually

1. Make Membership the Doorway to Involvement

One of the most counter-cultural principles of meaningful membership is that commitment to the church precedes formal involvement with it, not vice versa. Most churches view home groups and serving as slow on-ramps to the commitment of membership. However, that unwittingly undermines regenerate church membership.

It bypasses the congregation's role of affirming the person's testimony through baptism and membership, relying instead on a person's word and the private judgment of an elder or ministry leader.

Allowing formal involvement before commitment also implies that membership doesn't have much value. It teaches that remaining a Christian free agent is okay until you're comfortable and that membership is merely a procedural matter, not a biblical or spiritual one.

> "I don't think it's hyperbole to say that most Christians today think the local church is less important than God does."

I debated whether to include this item in the "immediately" or "eventually" category. It probably overlaps with both. I would *immediately* restrict "platform" involvement in corporate worship to members. However, it might be wise to roll out this principle more slowly regarding who can serve in certain ministries and participate in small groups.[6]

2. Institute Corrective Discipline

There's a temptation for new pastors to plow ahead in church discipline should a warranted case arise. But don't institute corrective discipline until you've had adequate time to teach and develop trust capital with your congregation. Moving too fast could cause the church to turn against you unnecessarily, but moving too slow could allow the cancer of unrepentant sin to destroy the church. Don't be hasty, but don't let the fear of man paralyze you either.

3. Address the Governing Documents

This one makes me chuckle because I led our church through a reconstituting process in the first four months of my pastorate. But my situation was unique. My predecessor had done the heavy lifting of a revitalization process.

Most of the time, addressing governing documents (statement of faith, covenant, bylaws) is a long-term project. But don't let the daunting nature of the task, or the time it might require, dampen your enthusiasm if it needs to be done.

Governing documents are massively important. They allow you to inject the DNA of meaningful membership more quickly and easily into the bloodstream of the church, and they make your church's public profile more appealing to those looking for a church with meaningful membership. Replacing bad governing documents is a good goal for the tail end of your first five years of ministry.

---

1. As opposed to "meaningful membership," which would describe a church made up of people who 1) have a credible Christian testimony, 2) attend the Lord's Day gathering regularly, and 3) understand the biblical privileges and commands entailed by participation at the Lord's Table (e.g. the "one another" commands of the NT).

2. At Redeeming Grace Church, I've preached a periodic series entitled The Disciplines of a Godly Church *(yes, it's a shameless knock-off of Kent Hughes's book title).* It's a Church Life 101-type of series. I've preached two sermons at a time from the series as a bridge between expositional series. Here are the ten sermon titles: Gather Together, Listen Together, Pray Together, Sing Together, Disciple Together, Serve Together, Evangelize Together, Submit Together, Give Together, Send Together.

3. Our standing requests are:
- Pray for the regular preaching and teaching of the Word.
- Pray for a warm culture of discipling and evangelism.
- Pray for the conversion of unbelievers who attend our services.
- Pray for our children and teens' salvation and growth in Christ.
- Pray for unity amid our diversity.
- Pray for wisdom and provision regarding our facilities.

4. Garrett Kell, "The Second-Most Important Book for Every Christian." TGC. July 2, 2014. https://www.thegospelcoalition.org/article/the-second-most-important-book-for-every-christian/.

5. The obvious exception is if your church doesn't have formal church membership when you arrive.

6. This statement assumes that your home groups are a programmatic way to encourage fulfilling the promises of the church covenant. Our church allows visitors to attend men's and women's Bible studies, as well as all worship and prayer services. But formal service and inclusion in our home groups are limited to members.

Jon Deedrick is the senior pastor of Redeeming Grace Church in Litchfield Park, Arizona. He also serves as director of The Gospel Coalition Arizona and as a board member of the Grove Church Planting Network.

Unique Temptations for a New Pastor

by Brian Parks

If you walked into our church seven years ago, the gray hair in my scruffy beard might have led you to mistake me for a veteran preacher. But despite some wrinkles and a penchant for 70's rock, I was a rookie. I had served as a lay pastor for several years and knew that leading a church plant would come with fresh challenges. But the new senior role exposed me to many temptations that I did not expect.

Some merely taunted and tempted me. Others I fell for.

Trying Too Much Too Soon

It's normal to begin with big vision and gospel-sized hopes for your church. But I was tempted to do too much, too quickly. Many weeks I succumbed and found myself overwhelmed, exhausted, and not doing anything particularly well.

"Better a patient person than a warrior, one with self-control than one who takes a city" (Prov. 16:32). Many weeks I set out to take the city but gained little ground.

All the parables with agrarian imagery also challenged me (cf. Mark 4:26–32). I've heard more than one wise shepherd suggest that pastoring is like farming; slow, faithful, day-in and day-out work bears the most fruit over time. The great preacher James Boice said that we usually overestimate what we can do in one year and underestimate what we can do in ten. Shorter weekly to-do lists and bigger long-term goals serve us well.

Focusing on Weak Sheep to the Detriment of Cultivating Leaders

Men with hearts like the Good Shepherd find great joy in taking care of the flock. And weak sheep will often ask for that care with greater vigor than members who occupy themselves with serving others.

In the early years of pastoring, I filled my time with caring for weak sheep and tended to neglect fellow or potential leaders. "We're doing more ministry if we spread our efforts, right?" I thought to myself.

But I forgot that God had called me to care for leaders as well. I needed to "entrust [the gospel] to faithful men, who will be able to teach others also" (2 Tim. 2:2). Jesus picked twelve and gave the bulk of his time, teaching, and training to them—even prioritizing Peter, James, and John among them. I needed to rethink the time I was investing in weak sheep in order to cultivate and care for fellow shepherds.

Launching New Programs Without Considering Long-Term Consequences

People love programs. If you can package and standardize ministry into events, it will often have greater appeal to people in your congregation.

Programs aren't bad in and of themselves. They often serve helpful purposes, whether it's Sunday morning classes, evangelism training, or youth group. Programs can serve God's purposes; the problem comes when they are seen as the *only* way to accomplish the goals for which they're designed.

The New Testament describes very few organized ministry activities in programmatic terms. Yet members have asked me on more than one occasion, "Why don't we have a _____ program?" Many of them had come from churches with programs galore. In Colin Marshall and Tony Payne's book *The Trellis and the Vine*, they tell of a church that had 23 different ministry programs listed in the bulletin every Sunday.

I often wanted the same goal that my members' proposed programs promised, but I feared that our goal would become perpetuating the program, over and against organic ministry in the lives of members.

Despite pressure from members, I was slow to implement new programs—while fortified by wise elders—and I'm glad for it. Ask yourself: are there ways to teach and train through your sermons, Sunday services, or other existing programs, instead of starting a new one? Would ordinary discipling relationships accomplish just as much as, if not more than, a new program? If the goal is to help people learn new ministry skills, might there be a short-term solution that won't saddle you with an ongoing program that could become a "sacred cow"? Think through long-term consequences before starting a new program.

Being Overly Buoyed by Praise or Sunk by Criticism

C.H. Spurgeon in his book *Lectures to My Students* says, "You cannot stop people's tongues, and therefore the best thing is to stop your own ears and never mind what is spoken." I return often to this chapter as I continue to pray for "thick skin" and a "soft heart," rather than the "thin skin" and "hard heart" that my sinful nature pushes me toward.

In my first years, I was overly buoyed by praise from members and overly discouraged by criticism. "That sermon really blessed me, pastor" is encouraging for anyone to hear, and we should praise God when it comes. But criticisms that catch us off guard can push us as low as praises take us high.

We serve the congregation, but Jesus is our master (1 Cor. 4:1). And it's to him that we ultimately answer. Here's where the temptation to neglect our own spiritual disciplines leaves us vulnerable to Satan's schemes. Regularly nurturing our discipleship and love of Christ guards us from being overly influenced by praise or criticism.

I follow English soccer with a passion. When new players make their debut, they're always vulnerable to "rookie mistakes," despite their skill and eager desire to serve the team. They'll make mistakes, alright! And many of the players learn from them and go on to become seasoned veterans.

The same is true for new pastors. If we navigate temptations with the Lord's help and humbly learn from our mistakes, the Lord will use us for his purposes.

I may have had gray in my scruffy beard, but in those early years of pastoring, Paul's words for Timothy felt like they were for me too: "Let no one despise you for your youth, but set the believers an example in speech, in conduct, in love, in faith, in purity. . . . Practice these things, immerse yourself in them, so that all may see your progress" (1 Tim. 4:12, 15).

Brian Parks is the senior pastor of Covenant Hope Church in Dubai.

Section Three

Over the Long Haul: The Middle Years

Prepare for Unexpected Storms

by Josh Manley

We planted the RAK Evangelical Church in Ras al Khaimah, United Arab Emirates eleven years ago. Since then, I have come to learn personally what I once knew only academically: God's Word is sufficient to safeguard God's church—even through the unexpected storms that you and your congregation will endure. Preaching effectively amid trials may seem daunting, but the Lord provides wisdom for how and what to preach.

Prepare by Trusting the Sufficiency of Scripture

Life in our fallen world is turbulent. Some members will be diagnosed with cancer, grieve over wayward children, or see new and wicked laws threaten their job security. Like people preparing for a hurricane with sandbags and boarded windows, pastors must ready their people for the storms that Scripture promises are coming (1 Pet. 4:12, Rom. 8:18).

The best way to prepare is to steadily exposit the Word of God in your sermons and Bible studies. Our preaching ministries should not just react to disappointment and tragedy. We should proactively apply God's enduring Word to the real and specific struggles of our members. The best time to prepare your people for suffering, persecution, or cultural marginalization is before they face them. The first time your people reckon with the sovereignty of God should not be when a storm hits.

For instance, this week my sermon text pointed to God's independence and immutability. These two attributes of God will help anchor my church in any storm ahead.

Good doctors don't just treat the sick—they equip people to pursue healthy habits. Our job is to serve as spiritual physicians, helping our flocks find nourishment and build theological muscle mass before disease cripples them.

Don't Assume Every Storm Affects Every Member

In our church, I've had the privilege of preaching to believers from Afghanistan to Zambia. Those saints have taught me that a storm battering Christians in one country may not rage in the same way elsewhere. While our brothers and sisters from the Philippines may have families picking up after a devastating typhoon, others fight the wicked actions of their oppressive nearby Middle Eastern government. But even in a church where most members share a common cultural heritage, pastors cannot assume that trials pressing hardest in some circles will press the same way in others.

Pastors should not react to every member's crisis from the pulpit. Yet we are called to share one another's burdens (Gal. 6:2). One way is to apply part of a sermon or study to situations on the minds of your people or set aside time during the pastoral prayer and church prayer meetings. You can pray for unemployment concerns, better education, or just laws. Because we are all members of one body, lead your body to care for each part without allowing the storms of a few to overtake the whole.

Persevere by Trusting God's Providence

Of course, everyone finds themselves in the middle of storms that engulf large parts of our church at once and would be pastoral malpractice to ignore—even when it's hard to see how highlighting the strife could possibly be edifying. As the Israeli-Hamas war began last October, it quickly became clear that this crisis was on the minds of everyone in our church, and it was provoking theological, political, and cultural questions. What can Christians agree to disagree on politically but not biblically? How do Christians think about war? Our elders agreed we should address these issues with the body.

Since our church lives together on the Arabian Peninsula, this particular conflict came with questions about war and peace for our region. These issues have been all-consuming for our members. Accordingly, I took time in our public worship to topically teach non-negotiables for every Christian navigating political differences—where the Scriptures bind our consciences and where there should be Christian freedom in the political sphere.

When big storms hit your entire church, they come with other voices that compete for your congregation's minds and hearts, and those voices are not always godly guides. Yet God has ordained you to be their pastor. You have the authority to apply God's Word to help saints weather the confusion, pain, and anger they're experiencing. Bringing God-given wisdom to bear in these cases is your job and privilege, and God will use you to care for his flock through challenges you never imagined.

Rest by Trusting That God Knows Your People's Needs

God knows the storms ahead, and he knows our members' needs better than we do. He loves them more than we do. The Lord reminds me of that regularly. Right now, for example, I am preaching the Joseph account in Genesis. And God used a sermon I preached a few weeks ago to prepare a family for suffering in the following days. What a joy to hear how that sermon helped them rely wholly on their sovereign God who reigns over confusing events in their lives.

> "God knows the storms ahead, and he knows our members' needs better than we do."

By his Word and Spirit, God enables us to address the unexpected storms before they hit.

Brother pastor, remember that the flock you have been called to shepherd is not your flock, but his (1 Pet. 5:2). They are safe in his hand (John 6:37–39). The great shepherd of the sheep is also the slain lamb who has conquered and rules all of history (Heb. 13:20; Rev. 5:5, 9). When the storms come, trust that not only has the Good Shepherd expected them, he has ordained them and equipped you with everything you need to faithfully shepherd your flock through them.

Josh Manley is the senior pastor of RAK Evangelical Church in the United Arab Emirates.

Raise up Leaders

by John Folmar

When I was a brand-new Christian, I remember wondering why Pastor Mark always insisted we go to Subway for lunch. How about some variety? Later on, I realized he was systematically building a relationship with the family behind the counter. He was also modeling intentionality and evangelistic faithfulness for me.

What Mark did for me is like what Jesus did with his disciples. He invested deeply in the Twelve and even more so in the Big Three (Peter, James, and John). It turns out this is a good model for any pastor trying to develop leaders—select a few promising men and invest deeply in them.

But what does this investment actually involve? Consider the following priorities.

1. Raising up Elders

In 2005, I accepted the call to be the pastor of Evangelical Christian Church of Dubai. There were six elders at ECCD when I arrived. They came from an array of theological backgrounds, including Brethren, Mennonite, charismatic, evangelical, and pragmatic. One elder also happened to be the pastor of a Mandarin-speaking church planted by ECCD. This conflict meant he never attended our church.

We were all over the place in our ministry philosophy and outlook. Some elders emphasized prayer walks, others organizational charts, others still Christmas shoebox ministry for the poor. These brothers were sincere, but the church was weak.

To turn the ship around, we needed theologically grounded elders who could "give instruction in sound doctrine" (Titus 1:9). I began to pray for men whose main concern was not program but equipping our members for the ministry of the church. I knew it was part of my job to see who God was working in and seek to raise those brothers up for pastoral ministry.

When a brother stood out from among the rest due to his love for the Word and our church, I would do any number of the following things:

- spend more time with him and get to know his character and family;
- read and discuss good books on theology (e.g., Packer, *Evangelism & the Sovereignty of God*), ecclesiology (e.g., Dever, *Nine Marks of a Healthy Church*), and counseling (e.g., Tripp, *Instruments in the Redeemer's Hands*);
- give him teaching opportunities where he could test his gifts (1 Tim. 3:2), such as Sunday evening prayer meetings or adult education classes;
- observe his ministry and fruitfulness in the church over time—especially his discipling relationships.

By God's grace, our church has since recognized 27 additional elders from eleven different nationalities. These men were diverse in ethnicity and cultural background, but increasingly united in doctrine and ministry philosophy. Serving alongside like-minded brothers like these is one of the greatest joys in ministry.

It's the Holy Spirit's job to make overseers (Acts 20:28). However, he often uses pastors to this end.

2. Discipling the Staff

When I arrived at ECCD, the church staff were not on the same page. They were affable, energetic servants who were involved in church life, but they lacked a theologically shaped ministry philosophy. To make matters more challenging, I was never given a leadership mandate. The former senior pastor was still in the church, though in a different role. This meant the staff did not recognize my authority in shaping the public services of the church. Some even mocked my leadership and scorned my proposals.

But over time, this too began to change. For one thing, I assigned good books. In 2006, we began with D.A. Carson's *The Cross and Christian Ministry* and Mark Dever's *Nine Marks of a Healthy Church*. Then we read and discussed the following:

- *Instruments in the Redeemer's Hands*, by Paul Tripp,

- *Evangelicalism Divided*, by Iain Murray,
- *Spiritual Depression*, by Martyn Lloyd-Jones, and
- J.I. Packer's Introduction to John Owen's *The Death of Death in the Death of Christ*.

The tide began to turn. These books gave the staff a shared vocabulary. I would ask questions about the argument of the book, and then we would apply the book's teachings to our ministry setting. Over time, these resources helped to shape our thinking in the areas of theology, pastoral ministry, counseling, and more. As a result, we grew in unity and ministry focus.

We also began weekly evaluations of our corporate gatherings. During Tuesday staff meeting, we would give specific feedback to everyone involved in the service—from preachers to service and song leaders to Scripture readers. These weekly course-corrections made us more ministry-minded and intentional in everything we did. It was especially useful for the staff to see me take seriously their criticisms and tips for improvement. Through their help, I became a better preacher. This exercise led to staff members growing spiritually, and we began pulling in the same direction.

3. Sending out Workers

Healthy churches often export surplus elders. Conrad Mbewe, who's church in Zambia has planted forty other congregations over the last three decades, has written, "It is the responsibility of church leaders to prayerfully identify those whom God is calling to this all-important work and to send them off."[1] Sometimes this means recruiting qualified candidates outside your church, training them, and appointing them as leaders of new work. More often, however, it involves recognizing qualified leaders the Lord has already raised up within your church. As two Australian pastors put it: "We should be talent scouts . . . constantly on the lookout for the sort of people with the gifts and integrity to preach the Word and pastor God's people."[2]

> "It's the Holy Spirit's job to make overseers. However, he often uses pastors to this end."

In Dubai, we've rerouted several church members into missions and church planting work, including:

- a former physiotherapist who now pastors an English-language church in the UAE;
- a former school tutor who now pastors a Russian-language church in Almaty, Kazakhstan;
- a former engineer who now pastors a German-language church in Munich;
- a former sales associate who now pastors a Nepali congregation in Kathmandu;
- a former security guard who now pastors a Hindi church in Bihar, India;

- most recently, a former honey-sales entrepreneur who aspires to pastor an Arabic-language church in the region.

These were all fruitful members of our English-speaking church who had first moved to Dubai for work. Over time, they began to give evidence of pastoral gifting—a hunger for divine truth, a love for God's people, an ability to teach, a positive spiritual impact on both church members and non-Christians. So we trained and redeployed them from within our church. The Lord of the harvest (Luke 10:2) had brought these men to ECCD, used ECCD to equip them, and then sovereignly redirected them.

When I first arrived in Dubai, I prioritized personal gospel outreach to people from the majority religion here. I spent lots of time evangelizing people at coffee shops, homes, or anywhere else I could interact with unbelievers. One time when I was back in the U.S. for a visit, a pastor asked me, "Are you spending time discipling and raising up future elders for the church?" It occurred to me that I had underemphasized leadership development, and that a long-term strategy of gospel growth required more leaders to shepherd the church and multiply our witness. One person can only do so much, but a whole church being led in the priority of evangelism can impact a city and the world.

Qualified leaders are crucial to healthy churches, and healthy churches are crucial to the advance of the gospel. In our case, it took years, but God raised up men from Asia, Africa, Australia, Europe, and America. Serving alongside them has deepened my faith, encouraged my soul, and helped to advance the gospel.

---

1. Conrad Mbewe, God's Design for the Church, 157.
2. Colin Marshall and Tony Payne, Trellis and the Vine, 139. See also the helpful list of qualities and characteristics that identify "people worth watching" on pp. 141–142.

John Folmar is the senior pastor of Evangelical Christian Church of Dubai in the United Arab Emirates.

Persevere in the Highs and Lows

by Clift Barnes

There is a certain beauty to the middle season of pastoral ministry. You find yourself between the zeal of your youth and the final stretch of your ministry.

Remember two things: First, there are highs and lows in ministry. I recall a pastor telling the story of a couple who, one Sunday, told him that his morning message was a home run; the following Sunday, they told him they were leaving the church. Seasons change.

Second, there is the need to persevere. As Paul tells Timothy, "Keep a close watch on yourself and on the teaching. Persist in this, for by so doing you will save both yourself and your hearers" (1 Tim. 4:16). The call to pastoral ministry is an extraordinary calling, where God graciously chooses what is "foolish in the world to shame the wise" in order to save eternal souls (1 Cor. 1:27).

To persevere is to be faithful to your commitment to the gospel of Jesus Christ. It is to fight the good fight, to finish the race, and to keep the faith (2 Tim. 4:7).

Persevere in the Highs

I know of a church that received a sizable financial gift that many pastors dream of. It was a sign of the Lord's kindness to them. In many ways, the gift made ministry easier.

Kind of. Christ's strength is still the secret to facing plenty and abundance (Phil. 4:12). In seasons flowing with milk and honey, we more easily forget our Deliverer (Deut. 6:10–12). Whatever the highs, what does persevering look like in the middle years? Here are some things to lean into.

Keep Maturing in the Ministry

If you have made it this far in the pastorate, you have most likely grown in ministering to others. The congregation has seen how God has sanctified you through different seasons. Praise him for it! He didn't leave you where you were!

Now consider your growth. Consider the growth of many in your congregation who have stayed. By what means did God mature you? Surely by beholding Christ in his Word, communing with him in prayer, fellowshipping with the saints, and obeying him even when it hurts.

Press in all the more. Highs in ministry can become ends in themselves and tempt you to strive after the wind. But continued spiritual growth will keep you from stumbling and being a distraction to the gospel. Look back to the mistakes you made in the zeal of your youthfulness and look forward to the blessing you want to be for the church after you leave.

Surround Yourself with Other Pastors

Ministers around you will be drawn to your example and experience. Younger pastors are looking for someone to imitate, and pastors near retirement are pushing others to finish well. Value the zeal of the youthful pastor and heed the elder pastor's advice.

Time in ministry has enabled you to establish solid relationships with others from both sides who can speak into your life with encouragement and exhortation. Continue to build upon those relationships.

Trust in the Grace of God

It is the Lord's grace that strengthens us to run with endurance. Never assume that the highs you experience are because "you have paid your dues." Laying a foundation and building upon it does take time, but the return is always in the Lord's hands. He brings about the increase. The privilege we have is to plant and water.

Persevere in the Lows

Imagine a mighty oak tree standing firm during a raging storm. The oak remains rooted in the ground despite the wind tearing at its branches and the rain beating it relentlessly. Ministry requires such steadfastness. James writes, "Count it all joy, my brothers, when you meet trials of various kinds, for you know that the testing of your faith produces steadfastness" (1:2–3).

When you experience lows in the middle years of ministry, and you feel like Joshua after the defeat at Ai or Jonah in the belly of the great fish, here are three reminders to stabilize you.

> "Imagine a mighty oak tree standing firm during a raging storm. Ministry requires such steadfastness."

Be Connected

The tendency for many during difficult times is isolation. I can remember wanting to keep to myself and hide the hurt. But I needed more profound and meaningful involvement and a more accurate picture of gospel community.

Be Vulnerable

Who are the people in your life to whom you can turn for guidance and wisdom? Be open with them about what you are going through. Trust those who have proven themselves trustworthy.

Be Holy

We are commanded to confess our sins (Jas. 5:16), and our shortcomings are magnified in the lows. Do not gloss over times of bitterness and resentment, but rather confess these things. What you do not talk out, you will act out. If you hold things in, sin will come out in ways that hurt the church.

Ministry in the middle years offers an opportunity to move forward while looking back at all that God has done. He is faithful to complete the work that he has started in you (Phil. 1:6).

Clift Barnes is the senior pastor of Horizon Christian Fellowship in El Paso, Texas.

Every Week I Preach My Guts out and... Nothing Changes

by David King

In your mythological mind's eye, behold Sisyphus. See him straining to roll a large boulder up a steep hill, only to have the boulder, just before reaching the top, tumble back down the hill. Immediately, he tries again with the same result.

As the story goes, Sisyphus is destined to relive this sad scenario for all eternity. How maddening to be on the brink of success and fall short again and again and again.

Preaching can feel like that. Every week, you push the rock up the hill, praying and preparing and preaching your guts out, only to feel as if you never reach the top. Maybe you hear "good job" and "that was helpful" and "thank you for all you do." But you can't help but notice some things:

- Unbelievers visit the church regularly yet seem unaffected by the gospel.
- Many church members remain marginally involved.

- Some wrestle with the same sins they've had for years.
- Marriages fail.
- Kids who grew up in the church walk away from the faith.
- Members leave over how you let them down.
- Prayer meetings are sparsely attended.
- Evangelistic zeal is minimal.
- The missional impact of the church seems negligible.
- The world continues to get worldlier.

It can seem as if your preaching changes nothing. The rock just keeps rolling back to the bottom of the hill.

The Sisyphean Lie

But is this really true? Is nothing actually changing? Even if our preaching is "out of season" (2 Tim. 4:2), God is always up to something through the faithful proclamation of his Word. Isaiah saw little fruit in his ministry, yet God assured him that the Word would not return empty but accomplish all that God had purposed for it (Isa. 55:11). It simply isn't true that *nothing* is changing when we preach, despite how we feel.

More likely, the problem is that we are looking for immediate and obvious results, not gradual and subtle ones. We want God to set off fireworks, but he's more interested in farming. Scatter the seed and go to sleep, Jesus said. Plant and water, Paul said. In time, God will give the growth (cf. Mark 4:26–29, 1 Cor. 3:6–8). The work of the Spirit through the preaching of the Word is about as explosive as watching a garden grow.

Examine your own trajectory of growth and be encouraged. Your timeline is likely punctuated with moments of rapid change—thank God for those moments! More commonly, though, you would probably testify your transformation has been slow. Do you think it's any different with the people to whom you preach?

In the words of Ray Ortlund, it takes time for people "to rethink their lives at a deep level, because people are complex and changing is not easy."[1] God ordinarily forms and reforms his people through his Word not in minutes or seconds, but in years and decades. Such slow change may be discouraging to us but not to him, with whom a thousand years are as one day. The results of your preaching may be unspectacular, but your labor isn't in vain. You aren't Sisyphus.

Where to Look

Still, the lack of apparent change can be disheartening. What should the preacher do when he's preaching his best but doesn't see fruit? I would suggest looking around, looking above, and looking ahead.

Look Around for Fruit That IS Present

I bet you are overlooking fruit. Is that senior saint persevering in the faith? Is that new Christian following Jesus despite the social cost? Is that single man looking for ways to serve? Is that mother content in caring for her family? Is that young adult considering missions opportunities? Let there be no doubt that the preaching of God's Word has contributed.

Just because the fruit is unassuming doesn't mean it's insignificant. Open your eyes to the simple work of God in people's lives.

Look above to God as You Preach

It's right to care about fruitfulness. We want God to use our preaching to save and sanctify. Regardless of the fruit, however, you can be satisfied knowing that you have been faithful to God. "Who is the faithful and wise servant," Jesus once asked, "whom his master has set over his household, to give them their food at the proper time? Blessed is that servant whom his master will find so doing when he comes" (Matt. 24:45–46).

Press on in faithful preaching—give the people their food at the proper time—and leave the results to God. Remember that you are ultimately speaking in Christ "in the sight of God" (2 Cor. 2:17), so render your service with good will "as to the Lord and not to man" (Eph. 6:7).

Look Ahead to the Day of the Lord

Presently, you cannot guess all the unseen work that God is doing through your preaching. But in the first light of eternity "each one's work will become manifest, for the Day will disclose it" (1 Cor. 3:13). On that day, if you have been faithful to preach Christ, you will see just how much God has used you in this world. I suspect you will be joyfully shocked.

Mowing in the Dark

Have you ever mowed your yard at dusk? You get home late from work, the sun is low in the sky, but you can't leave the grass uncut one more day. You fire up the lawnmower and get busy. In the fading evening light, it's difficult to see how well you're doing. Are your lines straight? Is everything being cut? Will there be scruffy patches that you missed? You've worked as carefully as you can. Now hang tight. Daylight is coming, and the morning will reveal all. (Let the reader understand.)

Keep on preaching faithfully. This present darkness may obscure the fruit of your labor, but the sun is about to rise.

---

1. Ray Ortlund, The Gospel: How the Church Portrays the Beauty of Christ *(Wheaton: Crossway, 2014), 72.*

David King is the senior pastor of Concord Baptist Church in Chattanooga, Tennessee.

Work Hard and Stay Hungry

by Juan Sanchez

It's exhilarating to watch the best athletes compete. They understand that the glory of a game is found in those who "leave it all on the field," whether they win or lose. So they train their bodies and develop their skills.

That is how I want to fulfill my ministry, as did the apostle Paul. He traveled from Jerusalem to Illyricum sharing the gospel and planting churches until he could say that he had fulfilled his ministry in those regions (Rom. 15:19). He preached the whole counsel of God, holding nothing back (Acts 20:26–27). Then, having fulfilled his ministry, he knew "the time of his departure had come" (2 Tim. 4:6). Paul left it all on the field.

If we're not vigilant as years in the ministry pass, though, the greater the possibility that the monotony of our routines, the burdens of pastoring, or the busyness of ministry will become excuses for neglecting our primary task: preaching the Word. Jesus builds his church by his Word, in the power of the Spirit, through the preaching of a foolish message, from

> "If we're not vigilant as years in the ministry pass, the greater the possibility that the monotony of our routines, the burdens of pastoring, or the busyness of ministry will become excuses for neglecting our primary task."

the mouths of weak men. Let us then work hard at preaching and stay hungry for the Word, remembering how we got here in the first place.

Remember Your Call

Paul viewed his call as both an obligation to God and a stewardship from God. The word "obligation" in Romans 1:14 is a financial term that can be translated "debt." While saved by grace alone, Paul understood he owed a debt of gratitude to God. This gratitude fueled Paul's ministry and zeal for the glory of Christ (Rom. 15:20).

Paul did not volunteer for this ministry. He did not choose his vocation. He was not set apart for the work by men.

He was called by God. By the grace of God, then, Paul was a steward of the gospel of God that revealed the Son of God (Eph. 3:1–2, 7–9). And he knew that one day he would give an account to the Master (Rom. 14:12).

Brothers, if we are to work hard and stay hungry, we must remember our call. Preaching is not a vocational choice; it is a calling. We are under obligation to preach Christ because God has saved us and set us apart for ministry as his mouthpieces. We are compelled to shepherd the flock of God among us by feeding Jesus's lambs with the Word of God.

Of course, none of us is sufficient for these things. Our sufficiency comes from the God who set us apart for ministry (2 Cor. 3:5). He alone is enough to get us to the finish line. But he is more than enough.

Struggling with All His Energy

Though Paul understood he worked only by the grace of God in him, he could still say he worked harder than anyone else (1 Cor. 15:10). Paul toiled to present everyone mature in Christ, "struggling with all [Christ's] energy that he powerfully works in me" (Col. 1:29).

The ministry to which God has set us apart is to preach the gospel. This gospel is the power of God for salvation (Rom. 1:16), the Word by which Jesus is sanctifying his church (Eph. 4:11–16). Brother pastors, to fulfill this preaching ministry we must do our best (cf. 2 Tim. 2:15).

The work of preaching begins with the work of preparation. That means communing with our Lord Jesus by his Word and prayer in reliance on the Spirit. Our ministry should be an overflow of our communion with the Lord. Ask God to maintain your hunger for his Word and a joy in his fellowship.

> "Like a good athlete, never stop training. Until you're in glory, you haven't arrived."

Second, we must prepare our sermon. Faithful preaching requires we work hard at "getting the text right." Be diligent to show yourself an approved workman in the task of exegesis, week in and week out. Ask as many questions of the text as possible, praying in the Spirit for illumination. Work to understand the context of the original audience, the argument the author was making to them, and how your text connects to the life-giving gospel. We have not prepared well until we know how to apply the sermon to the flock of God among us.

Third, like a good athlete, work hard at developing your "skill." In the words of Paul to Timothy, "do not neglect the gift you have" (1 Tim. 4:14). We should be constant readers. Reading cultivates a hunger for learning. We need to read all kinds of literature, not just theological books. For example, reading fiction stirs our imagination, which makes us better preachers. And reading non-Christian authors can provide insights into an unbeliever's perspective on human nature.

Finally, regularly evaluate your progress. Listen to your sermons and give yourself feedback. Invite others to give you feedback—maybe a group of local pastors or members of your church. Attend a Simeon Trust workshop. Consider the Chicago Course on Preaching. Pursue continuing education. Like a good athlete, never stop training. Until you're in glory, you haven't arrived.

Conclusion

Brother pastors, don't be complacent. Work hard and stay hungry. Remember your call. And struggle with all Christ's energy to preach the Word increasingly well, so that when you come to the end of your ministry you too can say, "I have fought the good fight, I have finished the race, I have kept the faith. Henceforth there is laid up for me the crown of righteousness, which the Lord, the righteous judge, will award to me on that day, and not only to me but also to all who have loved his appearing" (2 Tim. 4:7–8).

Juan Sanchez is the senior pastor of High Pointe Baptist Church in Austin, Texas.

Section Four

Passsing the Baton: Transitioning to the Next Guy

How to Decide When It's Time to Stay or Go

by Phil Newton

Leaving a pastoral charge can be hard. Staying can be hard, too. And deciding to stay or go is more complicated the longer one serves. Deep relationships, familiar patterns of worship, well-worn spiritual practices, and hard-won battles loom large before you.

In my autonomous church circle, the pastor, his wife, and maybe his closest friends are involved in the decision over staying or going. His elders or other leaders may become involved later. The pastoral process of staying or going calls for deep reflection, prayer, research, and waiting on God. What might that look like?

Aim for Longevity

Long pastorates give time to work through transitions in polity, leadership, worship development, mission impetus, and pastoral training. Short pastorates generally don't allow roots to grow deep among a people—roots that should make the thought of leaving feel like tearing up the heart's soil. So aim for longevity and then develop the following:

- *Develop a healthy spiritual walk.* A pastor lacks strength for ministry's rigor if he has failed to train himself for godliness, to devote himself to the Word and prayer, and to watch his life and teaching (1 Tim. 4:11–16).
- *Develop good roots in the congregation.* "Know well the condition of your flocks, and pay attention to your herds, for riches are not forever, nor does a crown endure to all generations" (Prov. 27:23–24). How will we "shepherd the flock of God," as Peter exhorted, without roots into the soil of their lives (1 Pet. 5:2)?
- *Develop attentiveness to the flock instead of the fence.* When struggling with pastoral matters, we can start gazing over the fence to find another flock. "Pay attention to your herds" can't happen if we're looking across the fence.
- *Develop contentment where the Lord has planted you.* Contentment frees us to focus on shepherding those entrusted to our care, for whom we will give an account (Heb. 13:17).

Remember Longevity Doesn't Mean Forever

Not all pastorates are long. Some end abruptly. But when you've stayed long, how do you know when it's time to move on?

First, You Must Have Self-Awareness

Would a vacation or sabbatical rekindle your pastoral juices, or are you at a point where you can no longer serve with joy but can't bring yourself to admit it? Have unpastoral attitudes affected your ministry patterns, requiring repentance and renewal? Are you reacting to wounds by a few causing you to think of leaving? Has pride gotten in the way of making a good decision about the future? Are your days of effective ministry in the past?

Second, You Must Be Realistic

Have you taken the church as far as they're willing to go? Have you exhausted your abilities to lead them? Would another pastor be able to better shepherd the flock in this season? Are you lagging in zeal, strength, pulpit passion, and leadership effectiveness, but reluctant to consider that a change might be best? Would retirement from active pastoral duties better serve your church, marriage, and life?

Third, You Must Be Reminded of Your Pastoral Charge

The church doesn't belong to you. Jesus called it "my church" when he committed to build it (Matt. 16:18). He may be pleased to use you for a season to accomplish his purposes, but that does not make you an owner. He may send you to plow and plant but raise others to harvest (John 4:35–38). Your pastoral stewardship involves the future as well as the present (1 Cor. 4:1–2).

> "The church doesn't belong to you. Jesus called it 'my church' when he committed to build it."

Therefore, hold your pastoral charge loosely. As difficult as it may be, faithfulness may require giving up that charge.

Ask Yourself These Additional Questions

When serving one congregation for an extended period, we develop perceptions that may affect our ability to discern whether to stay or go. Here are questions for further evaluation.

- Do you look forward to preparation for Sundays?
- Do you enjoy the rigors of shepherding?
- Do you sense joy when preaching?
- Are you able to patiently shepherd your people?
- Does your wife affirm your ministry?
- Do you have appropriate physical and mental health for pastoral work?
- Do you maintain adequate energy for the pace of pastoral ministry?
- Does your age significantly hinder your ministry?
- Are you able, with the elders' help, to keep up with the demands of shepherding?

Negative answers to any of these questions do not demand leaving! Again, you may need a good sabbatical to regain your passion and strength that could have weakened with a constant foot on the accelerator. Or you may need to realign staff and elder responsibilities. Or you may realize it's time to leave and entrust the flock to another shepherd. Assess yourself, confer with your wife and closest friends, and earnestly seek the Lord.

Prepare for Transition

If, after honest evaluation, you conclude that your church would be healthier if you stayed, then you must further ask yourself: Have I taught the church an unhealthy dependence upon my personality, gifts, and leadership style, rather than dependence upon Christ alone? If so, before considering a move, you may want to work toward increasing shared leadership, training members for ministry, and emphasizing Christ-dependence.

There's a sense in which pastors must always keep transition in the back of their minds. That may sound contradictory to the earlier appeal for longevity. But you don't know what divine providence might have for you. Therefore, labor to have your church healthy and maturing. Consider:

- Is the church in a healthy position so that if you suffered an accident, illness, or death, they're prepared to progress spiritually? We don't control life's narratives, divine providence does.

- Do you have confidence that the elders and staff can lead the church well in your unexpected absence? Train them in case of the unexpected.
- Have you been preparing the church for the day you go? Raise up faithful elders who can shepherd the church until it calls a senior pastor.

Utilize these questions to help you discern motives, perceptions, and readiness for you to stay or to go.

And if you do bid your flock goodbye, leave like a shepherd, not a hired hand.

Phil Newton serves as director of pastoral care and mentoring for the Pillar Network after pastoring for 44 years, the last 35 at South Woods Baptist Church in Memphis, Tennessee, which he planted in 1987.

Why Is It Hard for Pastors to Let Go?

by Sandy Willson

The title of this article is interesting. Why wouldn't a pastor be willing to let go of his ministry, let go of the burdens, let go of the committee meetings, let go of the crises? Why wouldn't he eagerly hand these things over to younger men?

There are a variety of reasons, some reflecting a godly sense of pastoral commitment and others reflecting a need to grow our trust in the Lord.

Sometimes, we pastors are reluctant to let go because we're not quite sure our congregations will prosper after we've departed, especially if unresolved conflicts or crises remain. In fact, a wise pastor will seek to retire when his congregation is in a particularly healthy season, so the church might more easily sustain the challenges of a pastoral transition.

But things don't always go as planned. I retired from Second Presbyterian Church on February 5, 2017. The very next day, I was on my way to Jakarta, Indonesia, when I received a call that one of our staff members was in an adulterous relationship.

In that moment, you can be sure that I didn't want to "let go" of my ministry at Second Presbyterian! But I did, because we had men and women trained to handle crises like this, and they, in fact, responded very wisely.

Sometimes pastoral transitions don't go well, and the previous minister struggles to let go when he sees his friends suffering. More commonly, pastors struggle to let go because of their own spiritual struggles. Here are the main ones I see from time to time.

1. The Pastor Is a Control Freak

Enough said.

2. The Pastor's Personal Identity Is Too Wrapped up in His Ministry

This is perhaps the most pernicious cause of not letting go. I hope young pastors and folks in full-time ministry are reading this. It is vital that our primary identity is as a child of God, not the leader of a ministry. Vocation comes before occupation. Our occupation is our means of gainful employment. Our vocation is our calling, which is to be in Jesus, to follow Jesus, to serve Jesus.

Every believer has the same calling, irrevocably given to us at conversion. We have many different occupations, which are determined by circumstances, wisdom, inference, and preference. All of these are eminently revocable.

> "It is vital that our primary identity is as a child of God, not the leader of a ministry."

We mustn't hitch our wagons to a job—any job, even pastoring. We must instead focus solely on our calling in Christ. The apostle Paul said, "I therefore, a prisoner for the Lord, urge you to walk in a manner worthy of the calling to which you have been called" (Eph. 4:1) and "to this end we always pray for you, that our God may make you worthy of his calling" (2 Thes. 1:11).

To whatever extent a person *needs* his occupation to provide an ultimate identity for himself, he has, to that same degree, abandoned his vocation. And this, of course, severely undermines his effectiveness in ministry and his ability to let go of the past and focus on the future.

3. The Pastor Did Not Prepare the Congregation Well for His Departure

Sometimes it's hard to let go because we leave too early. One reason it was relatively easy for me to let go of a 22-year ministry is because we had carefully planned my retirement with the welfare of the congregation in mind.

Our staff was strong, we entered a two-year period of training staff to lead in an interim period, and the congregation was content and at peace. I announced my retirement two years ahead of time, during which season we pledged to retire all our debt, we conducted an extensive church self-assessment, and we elected a high-quality search committee who began their work a year before I retired.

In short, I let go without a worry because we had planned so thoroughly.

4. The Pastor Did Not Plan His Next Ministry Well Before His Departure

Sometimes a pastor finds it difficult to let go of past ministry because he failed to plan for future ministry. He finds himself idle, underused, bored, and mildly depressed. He's already slept in several mornings, played extensively with the grandchildren, taken a couple of trips, reconnected with old friends, and even improved his golf handicap. But he knows something is badly missing, namely, the use of his pastoral gifts to serve churches.

Here's the good news: it's not too late. But the pastor who is looking back is unlikely to discover the most fruitful path of service forward. Three months before retiring from Second Presbyterian, I underwent training as an interim pastor that prepared me for the next seven years.

5. The Pastor Is Not Fully Trusting the Lord with the Future

When we pastors find ourselves reluctant to let go, even when we and our colleagues believe the time has come, it often reveals a deep deficiency in our spirituality, our theology, and our ecclesiology.

Spiritually, we have arrogantly fooled ourselves into thinking we are necessary for the ministry to flourish. Theologically, we have suppressed or forgotten the notion of God's eternal rule. Ecclesiologically, we have forgotten whose church this is. We are but Christ's servants.

As Moses reminds us, "The years of our life are seventy, or even by reason of strength eighty; yet their span is but toil and trouble; they are soon gone, and we fly away" (Ps. 90:10). It is a wonderful privilege to serve the Lord and his people in pastoral ministry. It is even more wonderful to lay it all at his feet with confidence, joy, and anticipation of a gracious and glorious future.

Sandy Willson is interim president of The Gospel Coalition. He is also pastor emeritus at Second Presbyterian Church, Memphis, Tennessee, after serving as senior minister there for 22 years.

Plan Your Transition

by Michael Indorf

"**E**verybody has a plan until they get hit in the face!" said boxer Mike Tyson, champion Joe Louis, and probably others. Getting hit in the face hurts, but having a plan doesn't need to be painful.

Some pastorates may feel like a fifteen-round boxing match. Whatever the situation, both boxing and pastoring have a beginning, middle, and end. As such, a faithful pastorate should include a plan for how to end and to transition to the next pastor. Yet that plan should connect to and not conflict with the providence of God.

Our Plans

In May 2023, I retired as the pastor of our church in Minnesota after serving there about fourteen years. Most of our family lived about 1000 miles away, and a few family members' health was beginning to decline.

> "A faithful pastorate should include a plan for how to end and to transition to the next pastor. Yet that plan should connect to and not conflict with the providence of God."

So my wife and I moved back to our home in Virginia. What follows is a brief account of the occasion in which I had a plan and, by the grace of God, witnessed a smooth transition to a successor.

By way of disclaimer, let me admit the obvious: not every plan pans out. I have heard plenty of stories of pastoral transition plans going pear-shaped. As you read about our transition, remember that no matter what your church's transition looks like, God is faithful and calls you to the same. He is praiseworthy in a smooth transition and a stormy one.

With that in mind, here is a brief overview of how my church moved on from my pastorate.

The Plan

About two years prior to my "retirement," I discussed our situation at an elder meeting. Privately, my prayer had been that I could disciple someone whom the congregation would recognize as the new senior pastor. Since that possibility did not appear imminent, the elders began to pray for God to connect us with someone whom we could recommend. We drafted a three-phase plan that extended over two and a half years:

Phase One (2–3 Years out, Elders Only)

- Collect an initial list of candidates from various trusted sources.
- Perform an initial screening of candidates.
- Conduct initial interviews by email, then in person.

Phase Two (1 Year out, Elders and Congregation)

- Notify the congregation of the transition plan.
- Announce my resignation by retirement "on or before" 12–13 months.
- Ask members to pray for our transition process and for wisdom and direction from God.
- Ask members to suggest potential candidates for consideration and review.
- Conduct detailed interviews and information exchanges with candidates.

Phase Three (3–6 Months out, Elders and Congregation)

- Solicit continued congregational prayer for the ongoing search.
- Announce the candidate recommendation to the church.
- Hold candidate meetings with the congregation.
- Schedule candidate preaching dates at the church.
- Recommend that the candidate serves as transitional part-time staff, pending congregational vote.

- Determine the transition period and an official retirement date.
- Schedule dates for a congregational vote on the candidate as senior pastor, then installation.

The Providence of God

If we were diligently working our own plans, did we actually trust God? Did God also have a plan? These questions are the concerns of providence.

We believe that God directs even the tiniest details by his providence. "The lot is cast into the lap, but its every decision is from the Lord" (Prov. 16:33). We believe God generally uses ordinary means, like plans showered in wise counsel (Prov. 15:22), as he directs providence. Of course, we also believe God is free to work outside of those same ordinary means. "Whatever the Lord pleases, he does, in heaven and on earth" (Ps. 135:6).

As we moved along the pathway of our pastoral transition plans, we prayed for God to direct our steps.

During Phase One, we asked God to help us be patient and wise in our conversations with various churches and networks. We decided to focus on young men who had some background in, or willingness to serve in, the upper Midwest. On several occasions, we invited seminary students to preach. This gave young men some valuable experience and gave us a feel for possible candidates. We praised God for how he helped us to meet new people and refine our sense of what sort of person we were seeking.

> "God generally uses ordinary means, like plans showered in wise counsel, as he directs providence."

Phase Two began with an announcement of my upcoming retirement. This took some people by surprise, leading to some questions and fears of the unknown. We encouraged our members that God was in control and reminded them of his care for us as his people. The fact that we were not proposing a typical interim period and search-committee process was a lot for the congregation to process. We urged members to trust God and to ask him for a smoother transition.

About three months after my announcement, I told a pastor friend in another city about our search. He said we should talk to a young man on his church staff.

In the providence of God, this man was completing his church planting residency and had a strong desire to minister in our city of all places. The two of us began having coffee every few weeks to discuss life and ministry. Over time, I saw this brother potentially as an excellent fit. Our elders prayed for wisdom and ultimately met with the man, presenting a phased offer of staff church planter to senior pastor, pending congregational approval. The brother flatly refused our offer because he wanted to start a new church, not serve an existing congregation.

Wait! How could this be the providence of God?

Our elders and the candidate agreed to suspend the conversation for two weeks so we could pray, seek counsel, and discern the will of God.

How was providence at work in the candidate? He shared:

I had resolved, with my family of six, to plant a church to the glory of God here in Mankato. We repeatedly had prayed that God would go before us, softening the hearts of those he had called us to reach. In his sovereign goodness, God indeed prepared a people for us, but in a surprising way that none of us anticipated.

I was stunned to receive an offer from the church, because I had told Michael for months about my church planting plans. But I agreed to prayerfully seek the will of God until the next appointed meeting.

Sometime during the following few days, I had an "out of the blue" call from a wise, seasoned pastor, precisely when I needed sound counsel. God used him, and like never before, the Lord made clear that he had brought us to this city not to plant but serve an existing congregation.

By the time we met again, God had given us all a strong, clear, and joyful unity of heart to move ahead together with our recommendation. Praise God!

Phase Three became a tremendous season of joyful thanks for our congregation to see the providence of God and receive this brother as a gift to serve and shepherd them for his glory. We rejoiced in Romans 8:28, "that for those who love God all things work together for good, for those who are called according to his purpose."

We had plans, and God in his kind providence led us all on the path of blessing.

Michael Indorf serves as interim pastor of White Stone Baptist Church near the Chesapeake Bay in Virginia.

Preparing a Church for Pastoral Transition

by William Spink, Jr.

The life cycle of a church includes a number of memorable milestones. One is pastoral transition. The longer a pastor has provided leadership, the more challenging the transition can be. That's why it's important to think carefully about how to navigate such waters.

I became pastor of my former church at the age of 27. Surrounded by a strong group of elders, I served the church for the next 39 years. Although it was difficult to imagine doing anything else, I knew that eventually I would need to step aside and allow the church to prosper under new leadership. But how would I go about that?

Transition Priorities

As I reflect upon the transition process we experienced, there are several key principles that came to the forefront.

> "The longer a pastor has provided leadership, the more challenging the transition can be. That's why it's important to think carefully about how to navigate such waters."

Number one, I was committed to "finishing well." In the strength of God's grace, I wanted to sprint to the finish line, not just coast in that direction. I wanted my final years to be fruitful, not a self-absorbed "victory lap."

Number two, I gave the church plenty of time to plan well for the transition. I offered the session (what we Presbyterians call our board of elders) a plan for my final two years which gave them time to form a search committee, develop a church profile, and communicate with potential candidates for the senior pastor position.

A third principle was the gradual transition of leadership from me, as senior pastor, to the session, as ruling elders. In God's providence, the clerk of the session assumed greater responsibility in leading meetings, making it evident that the session was becoming less dependent upon me.

A final critical priority was the need for open and frequent communication with the congregation. A familiar criticism of elders is the perceived lack of communication between leadership and membership. Pastoral transitions can produce great anxiety in the hearts of the flock. By regularly and carefully keeping the congregation in the loop, we tried to bless them with as much information as we possibly could.

Transition Insights

As I reflect upon the transition period in my church, I naturally ask, "What would I have done differently if I had to do it all over again?" Aspects could have been improved.

One possibility is that I might have "shared the pulpit" a bit more as my ministry approached its conclusion. Would it have prepared the congregation for a new voice if they heard less of mine in my final years? That might have been the case, but it was also important to me to keep the ministry "as normal as possible" in those final two years. Plus, we wanted to avoid giving the appearance of various preachers "auditioning" for the job before the search committee was actively at work.

Another important focus for me was emphasizing God's presence and faithfulness in the life of the church. My name had been connected to the church for 39 years, but it was not "my" church. It is God's church and has been built by God's power (1 Cor. 3:6–9). There was no need for the congregation to fear the future because God will faithfully build his church. That message had to be proclaimed repeatedly to avoid the natural inclination to look at the future with doubts.

Another important dimension of transition is the congregation's relationship with its departing pastor and his wife. The membership will wrestle with their emotions. Some feel rejected, others anxious, many are sad. The stages of grief may become visible in the faces of people you dearly love. The pastor and his wife may experience their own emotional challenges!

Admitting that these emotional dynamics exist and speaking into them is important. Pointing each other to the gospel and its promises is a powerful balm for ailing hearts. A transition should move in an orderly and proper fashion, but it should also offer emotional encouragement and biblical counsel to members who feel anxious about the future of the church they love.

The Story Continues

January 2020 was the official date of my "resignation" as senior pastor. The church survived the COVID-19 crisis that made church life difficult for quite a while. The search committee labored diligently and eventually identified a new senior pastor who has moved the church along with noticeable growth and blessing.

At the encouragement of wise advisors, my wife and I relocated for five months to a distant state so the church could process the separation without us being visible in the community. I believe that period of time was beneficial for all concerned.

Upon returning home, I became an interim preacher for another church within our presbytery. My wife and I have enjoyed almost four years serving that congregation. That assignment answered the important question of where we would be worshiping when we returned home.

In God's providence, our former church family recently extended me a call to return to the church in the role of pastor emeritus. The current senior pastor is enthusiastically supportive of the call, and we have been blessed to return to the congregation we so dearly love. I feel a great responsibility to steward that role humbly and faithfully so as to do nothing to compete with the new senior pastor or impede his ministry.

The life cycle of the church has come full circle. My wife and I had no idea when we arrived in 1981 that we would serve the same flock for 39 years. Nor did we expect to return in our seventies as pastor emeritus and wife! God richly blesses the church that he purchased with the blood of his Son.

William Spink, Jr. is a teaching elder in the Presbyterian Church in America. He pastored Riveroaks Reformed PCA in Tennessee for 39 years.

Support the Next Guy

by Doug Van Meter

As pastors prepare to retire, they should work hard to help the next guy succeed. A healthy transition to "the next guy" depends in part on "the old guy." He can support the incoming pastor or be a stumbling block.

It is customary for departing U.S. presidents to leave a letter for the incoming president providing encouragement and offering assistance. George W. Bush recently said that supporting Barack Obama meant being there for him as needed, but also staying out of the way. Healthy pastoral transitions often do best to observe the same principles.

This means the retiring pastor should do all he can to engage, encourage, and, at times, empathize with the new shepherd. Though pastoral transitions rarely depend upon "one size fits all" principles, everything that follows assumes a situation where the outgoing pastor is leaving well and supporting the new pastor. With this in mind, let's look at some ways that the old guy can best support the new guy.

Exit Happily

It's inevitable. Retirement means change. Even in the case of pastoral retirement, even when the retiree remains a member, his ministry to the church must radically change. He doesn't preach, counsel, lead the staff, or make the decisions like he used to. This is not an easy pill to swallow.

Retiring pastor, this means you have to let go. Make the commitment to happily respect the new pastor. Ask others to hold you accountable to support him in your private prayers and publicly among the congregation. Ask the Lord to give you contentment in your new role.

Engage Wisely

Supporting the new guy requires more than lip service in front of the congregation. It also means trying to be helpful to the new pastor. In some instances, the two pastors in transition will have a long-tested relationship built on trust. But even when this is not the case, it is vital that the older guy root for the younger guy. This means encouraging him and attempting to wisely engage so as not to be overbearing or completely absent.

Pastors in transition should spend time together even after the transition is over. They should dialogue and reassure each other. By doing so, the new guy will feel the support of the old guy and the old guy will be comforted in his new stage of ministry.

Spending time together also creates an opportunity for sharing about various pastoral situations in the church.

> "The retiring pastor should do all he can to engage, encourage, and, at times, empathize with the new shepherd."

The old guy can equip the new guy to fruitfully shepherd those in the congregation who are weak, anxious, prickly, or just need extra oversight.

To the retiring pastor, take the initiative to have conversations, but don't push it. Let the new guy know you're available, but don't force open the door.

Encourage Faithfully

Paul instructed the Roman church, "Love one another with brotherly affection. Outdo one another in showing honor" (Rom. 12:10). This is a good principle for pastors in transition. Though there might be areas of disagreement, the former pastor should see his role as an encourager.

If the retiring pastor remains a member, he should visibly support the new guy. Non-verbal nodding in agreement and verbal "amening" can go a long way.

Empathize Appropriately

New pastors eventually reach the end of their "honeymoon" phase in a church. Problems mount and discouragement presses in. When those hard times come, the retired pastor, knowing how hard ministry can be, should show empathy for the new guy.

From the get-go, he can be a sympathetic listener, a prayerful friend, and a wise counselor. He may occasionally need to speak the truth in love, but this should normally be done with gracious deference.

Conclusion

At the end of his ministry, Paul left a letter for pastor Timothy. He wrote, "You therefore my son, be strong in the grace that is in Christ Jesus" (2 Tim. 2:1).

This is necessary counsel for both new and retired pastors. By clinging to the gospel of the grace of God, the former pastor can have a happy exit, the new pastor is equipped for a happy succession, and the congregation is well-positioned for a healthy continuance.

Doug Van Meter is the senior pastor of Brackenhurst Baptist Church in South Africa.

How Should I Serve My Church after I Stop Being Its Senior Pastor?

by Bob Johnson

The year 2024 marks my 35th year as the senior pastor of the same church. I'm about to turn 64. After I step away, how should I be involved in my church?

I'm faced with lots of options: leaving completely, remaining as a staff pastor with a different role, and everything in between. I don't know what my future will look like, but I do know a few truths that will inform my answer.

1. The Local Church Is Bought by Jesus

It may feel like my church, my flock, my people, my family—and in some ways it is. But ultimately, this local church does not belong to me. It belongs to Jesus, and I am seeking to keep it true to its purpose during my stint at the helm. Therefore, my job is to be faithful to the Chief Shepherd, not to influence the life of the church around "my ministerial career."

> "It may feel like my church, my flock, my people, my family—and in some ways it is. But ultimately, this local church does not belong to me."

A friend of mine asked if I had given any thought to what my last expositional series would be. I think that is the wrong way to look at it. The last series of sermons I preach should be the next series the congregation needs to look more like Christ.

Meanwhile, I need to refrain from reminding people how long I've been here, or from nostalgic references that draw undue focus to me. The church will be fine without me. It belongs to Jesus.

2. My Membership in the Church Is Directly Related to My Union in Christ

In my heart of hearts, I am a follower of Christ. I am a member of his church because I am in him. This means that I see myself fundamentally as one part of this congregation. I am not a member here because this is my job. My role in the church is grounded in my membership in the church. I need to look at my role now and the inevitable transition through the lens of what is best for the body to which I've been united.

3. The Needs of My Church Will Determine What Role I Take

When I step away from this role, the church will have needs that may be different than what they are today. I need to ask the question every member should ask. What does my church need and how can I help meet that need?

The elders may determine I should stay formally engaged on the elder board to give confidence to the congregation about the change. They may determine I should attend another church for a while to give the change time to happen outside of my shadow and to build the congregation's trust. They may want me to serve other churches in some capacity. We may need another guy on the grass-cutting crew, or greeting, or singing bass in the choir. This next season will give me an opportunity to be an example of a faithful member who serves because he loves Jesus, not because he gets paid.

So . . . how should I be planning on what my future will look like?

I need to pray for a humble heart that honestly desires affection and attention to Christ.

I need to remind the congregation that the day will come when I will not be in this role. I want the topic on the table so the congregation knows I am comfortable with it and so they can be comfortable with it.

I need to help the elders lead the congregation in what the transition process will look like.

I need to lead the congregation to pray for the next brother and the elders as they map out a transition plan.

> "I need to ask the question every member should ask. What does my church need and how can I help meet that need?"

I need to share the pulpit, and not just when I am out of town. The congregation needs to see me hearing other brothers preach and loving it.

I need to be ready to support and encourage the brother who takes my place. While people are kind and gracious, the truth is, every leader quickly becomes "ole' what's his name." I need to deal with that in my heart now and prepare to be the next brother's biggest prayer supporter.

I need to enjoy God's grace every day and realize that, as I step away from this role, I can savor these new opportunities.

Bob Johnson is the senior pastor of Cornerstone Baptist Church in Roseville, Michigan.

Section Five

Finishing the Race

Six Lessons I Learned When I Could Not Pastor

by John Erickson

I trust we all dream of having long, faithful, and fruitful pastoral tenures.

At the last T4G, tears came to my eyes when Mark Dever asked pastors who had served for decades to stand. I wanted to be one of those pastors and to do nothing more than pastor the church we planted in 2009. The church was in the neighborhood I had grown up in, three blocks from my high school.

But God had other plans.

2020 was difficult everywhere, but, watching our Minneapolis neighborhood burn, the year felt particularly challenging for my congregation. It became a year of crisis counseling. Deaths in our family added to the strain, and by the end of the year, my health broke down. I was bedridden, and my doctor had no answers.

For over a year I did not recover and was unable to work. My health did not return, and I had to resign.

I was surprised by this fiery trial. I didn't know if I would get better; I didn't know *how* to get better. How would I provide for my family?

By his grace, God restored my health, but only after I was no longer a pastor. So, I began a new season of listening to other men preach.

Here are six lessons that may strengthen you when your fiery trial comes.

1. More Child Than Pastor

Almost every conversation I have with pastors moves quickly to any suffering they are experiencing. Scripture tells us not to be surprised by the fiery trials, yet I was.

It's an odd reality to no longer be a pastor—to not be Pastor John and not preach God's Word week after week but instead listen to others. Yet this transition comes for each of us. When it does, we wrestle with who we are. Pastoral ministry significantly defines how we see ourselves.

For me, it was a journey of growing deeper and deeper in the knowledge that before I was a pastor for God, I was his child. Our great God is with us. He leads his dear children along. When I could do little else, I sought to learn new hymns. One that became so precious is "God Leads Us Along."

In shady, green pastures,
so rich and so sweet,
God leads his dear children along;

Though sorrows befall us
and Satan opposes,
God leads his dear children along;
Through grace, we can conquer,
defeat all our foes,
God leads his dear children along.

Some through the waters,
some through the flood,
Some through the fire,
but all through the blood;
Some through great sorrow,
but God gives a song,
In the night season and all the day long.

These words seem so simple. Amid many tears, they were a balm. I had to wrestle with this transition. Pastoral ministry is not who we are. It is a wonderful role, but whether or not we are pastors, we are his children, and he is our kind Father.

2. There's Joy to Be Had in Steadfastness

In suffering, familiar verses become freshly challenging. "Count it all joy, my brothers, when you face trials of many kinds" (Jas. 1:2). Not being able to pastor, not being able to provide, and not knowing how to get better—or if I ever would—were things I found hard to count as joy. Yet meeting with our good Father morning by morning, he was gently teaching me the next verse: "For you know that the testing of your faith produces . . ." What was God producing? Steadfastness.

What is steadfastness? It's a military term that means to stand fast, not to turn to the right or left, not to quit or surrender, lay down, or run away. As I thought about my life's ambition, I knew one of my deepest desires was to be able to say with Paul in my last days, "I have fought the good fight, I have finished the race, I have kept the faith" (2 Tim. 4:7). God desired my steadfastness to grow through this trial.

> "Pastoral ministry is not who we are. It is a wonderful role, but whether or not we are pastors, we are his children, and he is our kind Father."

Amidst extended sickness, I found myself standing next to my 6'8" son in a lake as he was about to be baptized. The first line of his testimony nearly wrecked me: "As I have watched my dad walk through this season of suffering, it has clarified for me the importance of faith in Christ." At that moment, I knew that health was not my greatest need.

3. Preaching Blesses the Humble Hearer

It's a great honor to preach Christ. We have the words of life. What a stewardship it is to be heralds of such words. Go on preaching Christ. When saints in tears come to say thank you for preaching Christ, it is an unspeakable honor. When you can no longer do so, that stewardship becomes more evident.

We have this ministry by the mercy of God. Our great God doesn't need any of us, yet in his kindness, he has invited us to participate in the most significant victory in history. It is a great joy when your church continues in health and joy, and it is humbling that your church continues without you. Our ministries are not unimportant, but Jesus builds his church with or without us.

It's humbling not to be the preacher. And yet, as we sit week after week under other men, we are hearing the Word of God. I had to learn to turn down the volume of critique and instead listen as one addressed by God in his Word. The path of humility is the path where God gives grace.

4. Whate'er My God Ordains Is Right

In the fiery trial, in our unanswered prayer, when biting criticism comes, we rest in the powerful old truth: whatever my God ordains is right.

There are moments we simply don't understand. Yet we know God, and we know that he does. We don't need every question answered; instead, we need confidence that our Father is good, that he is ruling and reigning, and that he is with us for good.

In 1675, Samuel Rodigast penned these words,

Whate'er my God ordains is right:
his holy will abideth;
I will be still, whate'er he doth,
and follow where he guideth.
He is my God; though dark my road,
he holds me that I shall not fall:
wherefore to him I leave it all.

Whate'er my God ordains is right:
though now this cup, in drinking,
may bitter seem to my faint heart,
I take it, all unshrinking.
My God is true; each morn anew
sweet comfort yet shall fill my heart,
and pain and sorrow shall depart.

May our Father strengthen us to rest in these vital truths.

> "Our great God doesn't need any of us, yet in his kindness, he has invited us to participate in the most significant victory in history."

5. Communion Is Worth Fighting For

Pastoring is very public work. Many listen to you week after week. They talk to you. They know you. When that stops, it is strange. Now you are a hearer. You are listening and not speaking. Yet in this private place, the repeated echo of Matthew 6 can be heard, "your Father who sees in secret."

I am learning more about a life lived with my Father in secret—not sinful isolation, but a life of *coram deo* before the face of God. Don't wait until after pastoral ministry. Press in now. Our Father invites us to commune deeply with him.

We must fight for this communion. Howard Hendricks did research years ago on pastors who fell into moral failure. The one practice he found they all had in common was that they had stopped personal devotional time in the Word of God. They were going to the Bible only to prepare. Hudson Taylor says, "Communion with Christ requires our coming to him. Meditating upon his person and his work requires the diligent use of the means of grace, and specially the prayerful reading of his Word. Many fail to abide because they habitually fast instead of feed."

Brothers, this seems obvious, yet your enemy will never stop seeking to distract you with many other things. My prayer is for a Psalm 105:4 heart, "Seek the Lord and his strength, seek his presence continually."

6. Better Written in Heaven Than Used on Earth

Brothers, what a great thing to be a pastor. What a joy it is to be used mightily by God. Yet there is something more significant. We can learn from Martin Lloyd-Jones and Tim Keller. In his last email to John Piper, Keller recalled that the last text Lloyd-Jones reveled in was Luke 10:20, "Nevertheless, do not rejoice in this, that the spirits are subject to you, but rejoice that your names are written in heaven."

Brothers, ministry success is a gift, but even better, our names are written in heaven. Suffering focuses our vision on the glory to come, oh what glory! Rejoice with the Doctor, Keller, and King Jesus that in the midst of all that you are going through, our names are written in heaven.

John Erickson was a pastor and church planter for 25 years and is now pastoring pastors for the Treasuring Christ Together Network.

Learn to Rest

by Wes Pastor

There's a time to pastor and a time to rest.

Thirty-three years ago, in January of 1991, my wife Sue and I moved with our four children to Burlington, Vermont. After nearly two years of recruiting, Christ Memorial Church was born on September 13, 1992. It was a time to pastor.

In the fall of 2021, after leading the church for over thirty years, I turned over the reins to my successor. It was a time to rest.

But how does one stop doing what he has loved for over three decades and spent most of his life preparing for? How does one who witnessed the birth of something so glorious walk away? How do you fight the good fight for so long and then retreat from battle?

Simply put, you don't. Not when you know countless souls are still headed for hell. Not when you hear of churches struggling with barely a pulse. Not when scores of church buildings are being converted to condos and delis and town meeting halls in your neighborhood, and throughout New England

and the Northeast. You don't when there is still juice in the tank to serve.

How can the proverbial old dog learn to rest? The key is in not retreating completely. It's to not kill the engine of life, but to downshift one's responsibilities, as in parenting. When Sue and I host grandkids for an overnight, by the time they leave, we look at each other and say, "How did we ever do that 24/7 with our five kids?"

Senior pastoring is a young man's game. The physical vigor, the mental stress of leading, vision-casting, counseling, and preparing sermons is demanding. At some point, you have to let that go. Just like you don't completely stop parenting, you don't completely stop ministering. It just looks different.

So I've downshifted my responsibilities. I've let go of being a lead pastor and the daily stress of managing a local flock. But what does it look like to downshift? To rest? Here are four things I'm trying to do at this stage of ministry.

1. Serve Christ's Church

This is done both formally and informally, but my goal is to bless the church with what I've learned over a lifetime of ministry. Though no longer senior pastor, I continue to serve at Christ Memorial as a minister-in-residence—counseling, preaching, leading a community group, teaching Sunday school, and serving as a mentor and resource to the other pastors.

In addition, I'm blessed to continue as president of The New England Training and Sending Center for Church Planting and Revitalization (NETS), a ministry of Christ Memorial for the last 24 years. This keeps me quite busy, preaching at NETS Network churches, recruiting at seminaries, mentoring pastors in the field, training and placing church planters and revitalizers in New England and beyond, and ministering to churches throughout New England, the U.S., and abroad.

I'm also pursuing ministry avenues I didn't have time for as a senior pastor. In April, NETS will launch a podcast for pastors called *Pastor Pastor*. I'm working on my first book, a goal I've had for over a decade, and have other book ideas in the queue. There's much to be done, even at rest.

2. Study God's Word

Again, this is both formal and informal. Though previously accepted into two Ph.D. programs, I could never matriculate due to pressing responsibilities at Christ Memorial and NETS. The month after I resigned, I began Ph.D. work at Midwestern Baptist Theological Seminary and am on track to finish next year. It's been rich and rewarding, caused me to stay in the game with my Greek, and began resurrecting my Hebrew. I'm hoping to add to the body of knowledge on progressive sanctification from the position that takes Romans 7:13–25 as an unbeliever, a perspective that has significantly shaped my shepherding.

My own time in the Word and prayer has also increased, especially in the Psalms. It has greatly ministered to my soul to see my Savior throughout the Psalms in new ways. And the freedom to linger a bit over Scripture and chase down questions that time did not permit in the past has been a blessing.

3. Engage Family

God has blessed Sue and me with five believing children, all happily married. He's also blessed us with seventeen grandkids, fourteen girls and three boys. Retiring from the pastorate means Sue and I can drop everything when they visit (like just now, when our two-year-old grandson came by) and can take the grandkids for more overnights. We recently bought a used 28-foot RV that will sleep four kids. We're looking for ways to be a bigger part of their lives, as well as to bring the families together.

Sue and I spend time together in the evening. As senior pastor, my evenings were taken up with ministry. We're currently watching the TV drama *West Wing*, complete with popcorn and analysis (and catching up on emails). God has shown me great favor with a dear wife and growing family, and now there's more time to enjoy them.

4. Pursue Other Interests

My commitment to the church these last three decades meant spending less time pursuing other activities I enjoy. With the purchase of this RV, Sue and I plan to tour some national parks and historic landmarks in Vermont and New England. I recently became a trumpet sub for the Vermont Jazz Ensemble (my dad was a professional trumpet player and I played in college). I'm hoping to land a permanent spot in the group, Lord willing.

And 31 years ago, God blessed us with a large fixer-upper home. Now, after three dogs (and a dog-breeding business), one cat, several guinea pigs, and five kids, we've begun in earnest to upgrade this old house.

During COVID, we redid the kitchen, much to Sue's delight. Now we're looking at remodeling the second floor, the only area that has remained largely untouched. Sue has contentedly done without for decades. Having paid for wrecked cars, college degrees, and all or part of five weddings, we now have some discretionary funds. I'm eager to bless my faithful ministry partner with a new master bedroom and bath.

Sue and I are learning to rest with responsibilities consonant with our age and energy levels. Although enjoying what God has given is certainly not wasteful (1 Tim. 4:4–5), as John Piper said, we must not waste our retirement. May our heavenly Father be pleased with the sacrifice we offer as we serve him diligently in this final chapter of our lives (Rom. 12:1–2).

Wes Pastor is the founder and president of The NETS Center for Church Planting and Revitalization, and founding pastor and pastor emeritus of Christ Memorial Church in Williston, Vermont.

Pastor, Remember Where Your Identity Is Found Before You Retire

by Phil Newton

John Newton, former slave trader turned minister and hymnwriter, lay dying. Barely audible, he uttered, "My memory is nearly gone, but I remember two things: that I am a great sinner and that Christ is a great Savior." He made no mention of extraordinary hymns he wrote, or sermons he preached, or men he mentored.

A great sinner. A greater Savior. That's what lingered in John Newton's mind when he faced eternity.

That keen focus on eternity didn't start as he lay dying. Newton had long labored to keep his eyes on Christ and eternity, rather than fame and adulation. He didn't see himself, or pastors in general, as indispensable. We can hear this in his letter to John Ryland Jr. about Andrew Fuller's serious illness:

> I hope that he and you and I shall all so live, as to be missed a little when we are gone. But the Lord standeth not in need of sinful man. And he sometimes takes away his most faithful and honored ministers in the midst of their usefulness

perhaps [for this reason] among other reasons, that he may show us he can do without them.[1]

The Lord can do without us. And yet in his wise purposes and for his good pleasure, he appoints us *for a season* to shepherd a little portion of his flock until he's ready to appoint another.

We may nod agreeably at that sentiment. But living it—pressing on in life after letting go of a pastoral charge—is quite another challenge. Pastoral ministry brings unmeasured joys and opportunities, challenges and trials. Nothing quite compares to it. However, if our identity is preaching and pastoring, what happens when we no longer stand before people to preach and pastor? We must labor to have our identity fixed on Christ and eternity with him.

I recently heard Matt McCullough tell fellow pastors, "We're pilgrims being formed for heaven." We're not only readying others for heaven. We're on that journey. We must get our eyes on the destination and not linger too long on the preparation. Consider a few helps in this pilgrim journey.

Familiar Patterns in Ministry

Pastors spend countless hours doing their jobs. Twelve to twenty hours a week in sermon preparation is normal. Hours spent counseling members, preparing for worship gatherings, and interacting with fellow pastors fill a week. Pastors begin and lead new ministries. They show up at the hospital after a happy birth. They show up at the hospital after a surprising death. They rejoice and they comfort. They do premarital counseling and plan a wedding ceremony. They travel out of town for the wedding weekend. They counsel and pray for someone trapped in sin. They meet with fellow elders to pray, plan, and mobilize care for the flock. Rarely do pastors accomplish all they hoped in a given week.

> "The Lord can do without us. And yet in his wise purposes and for his good pleasure, he appoints us for a season to shepherd a little portion of his flock until he's ready to appoint another."

Then we stand before our people on Sundays; their eyes and ears are locked on us. We receive their comments, greet them at the door, see wounds in their eyes, and listen to sins confessed. We share joys and sorrows. We point them to Christ, but we know how easy it is to become the center of our congregation's attention. They know us. They trust us.

And then we leave. That's when reality hits.

Reality Settles In

Suddenly, you announce you're stepping down, and you're no longer at the forefront. Your wife is no longer the church's "first lady." You no longer get calls asking for your counsel. You're not the first to know about an ER visit or baby born. No longer do you hear the knock at the study door. You once thought of this as an interruption, but now you long for it, missing how often someone found encouragement from your counsel. You no longer lead worship gatherings or staff meetings. You don't direct the church's mission or budget. You're no longer the man everyone looks and listens to.

If your pastoral position has become your identity, then get ready for despondency to follow. Get ready for lethargy and restlessness to strike. You can only pull so many weeds from your garden to distract your thoughts from the aimlessness you feel. That is, unless you've prepared.

A Better Way

If we wisely prepare, then stepping out of the lead pastor's limelight will feel more like reaching a mountain's peak as opposed to stopping mid-ascent. Consider three practices to reshape pastoral identity.

First, Focus on the Eternal

"We're pilgrims being formed for heaven." When returning from their ministry assignment, filled with elation over successfully exercising their gifts, Jesus told the seventy-two, "Do not rejoice in this, that the spirits are subject to you, but rejoice that your names are written in heaven" (Luke 10:20).

Yes, we point people to heaven as a normal duty, but do *we* meditate on heaven? Do *we* long to see Jesus face-to-face? Do *we* discipline ourselves to "set [our] minds on things that are above, not on things that are on earth" (Col. 3:2)?

Make this focus on heaven a regular part of your prayer and meditation.

Second, Aim to Keep the Faith

Some grow crotchety late in ministry, others cynical. That wasn't Paul's heart in 2 Timothy 4:7: "I have fought the good fight, I have finished the race, I have kept the faith." He persevered through massive struggles in ministry. He kept the faith.

Do we keep the faith? Do we daily consider the promises of Jesus secured in the gospel and rest in them by faith? Do we progress in trusting Christ? That kind of perseverance in the faith prepares us for whatever God's providence hands us.

Third, Be Steady in Your Christian Walk

As Peter ended his second epistle, he turned to the reality of Christ's return, and with it, the cataclysmic reversal of everything touched and affected by the fall. With that in view, he counseled, "You therefore, beloved . . . take care that you are not carried away with the error of lawless people and lose your own stability. But grow in the grace and knowledge of our Lord and Savior Jesus Christ" (2 Pet. 3:17–18).

Observe four practices that fix identity on Christ and eternity: (1) Remember the judgment that follows Christ's return. (2) Avoid licentious patterns. (3) Remain steady in habits of trusting and obeying Christ. (4) Keep growing in the grace and knowledge of Christ.

> "The habits and patterns of our spiritual focus in the present will prepare us for the day when we're not front-and-center."

Fourth, Remember You're a Church Member Before You're a Pastor

You did not begin life as a pastor. Christ met you in saving grace. In his mercies, you became part of a church body through baptism and their welcome. By the Lord's kindness, the local church nurtured you in the faith and affirmed your ministry call. Return to your roots in the church as a member who loves and encourages his pastors, who prays for fellow members, and who readily serves as you've called others to do for years. Perhaps, as a member, you'll help nurture and affirm a young man who will pastor as you did.

The habits and patterns of our spiritual focus in the present will prepare us for the day when we're not front-and-center. Will we miss it? Probably so, but if we've learned to focus on eternity, keep the faith, and remain steady in our Christian walks, then when that transition comes, it's just that: a transition, not our demise.

Pastoral ministry is not ultimate. It's far sweeter to taste this reality: we are great sinners with a greater Savior.

---

1. Grant Gordon, ed., Wise Counsel, 280

Phil Newton serves as director of pastoral care and mentoring for the Pillar Network after pastoring for 44 years, the last 35 at South Woods Baptist Church in Memphis, Tennessee, which he planted in 1987.

Brothers, Train up the Next Generation

by Mike Bullmore

I find there is a persistent temptation in my life and ministry—the temptation to just finish my own race faithfully.

"What's wrong with that?" you ask. It sounds fairly biblical, almost Pauline. "I just want to finish the race. I don't want to be disqualified but be found faithful to the end." Which is well and good, *unless* the understanding of faithfulness to the gospel is limited to my allotted three score years and ten, or if by reason of strength, four score.

I don't know about you, but the challenges and weight of pastoral ministry can sometimes reduce my ambitions to, "Lord, just help *me* to be faithful to the end."

On the flipside of that temptation is the fact that maintaining a passion for the future can be difficult, especially a future beyond our sight. It's easy to be passionate about my children's well-being or even their children's well-being. But it's hard to maintain that passion much beyond three generations without falling into abstraction.

I share all this to say, it's easy to regard something as good as gospel faithfulness too much in terms of our own tenure. What we need, therefore, is to view *faithfulness in gospel ministry as including an investment in what comes after us.*

Disciple Faithful Men

Paul tells Timothy, "Guard the good deposit entrusted to you" (2 Tim. 1:14). A few verses later, he explains that guarding includes entrusting to faithful men what had been entrusted to him, men who would in turn pass it along to others (2 Tim. 2:2).

An essential part of faithful gospel ministry, in other words, is investing in the next generation. It is not an optional add-on. In other words, when Paul tells Timothy to "guard" the gospel, he is not merely calling Timothy to protect the integrity of the gospel from false teaching. He is also calling Timothy to fight to preserve the continuation of the gospel against the effects of erosion over time, even beyond Timothy's time.

So let me say it again. *Essential to our faithfulness in gospel ministry is investing in a succeeding generation of gospel ministers.*

Beware Hezekiah Syndrome

I believe the greatest challenge to being mindful of such investment is the "my lifetime" tendency, a tendency we see exemplified in King Hezekiah of Judah. When the prophet Isaiah predicts that a Babylonian captivity will occur after Hezekiah dies, Hezekiah replies, "The word of the Lord that you have spoken is good." Then he thinks, "There will be peace and security in *my lifetime*" (Isa. 39:8).

What makes this account even more sobering and a warning to us is the fact that Hezekiah was extremely influential in reforming the spiritual life of Judah. He cleansed the temple, restored temple worship, reinstated Passover, and reorganized the priesthood. He made an impressive contribution.

But this late-in-life episode reveals his pride and myopia. Despite his zeal for God's house, apparently he wasn't zealous about what happened after he passed off the scene.

Avoid Temporal Shortsightedness

Richard Baxter addresses our shortsightedness wonderfully in *The Reformed Pastor*. He writes, "If you will glorify God in your lives, you must be chiefly intent upon the public good, and the spreading of the gospel through the world." The alternative is "a private, narrow soul always taken up about itself that sees not how things go in the world. Its desires and prayers and endeavors go no further than they can see or travel."

Baxter points to a geographical shortsightedness, but we might also be guilty of a temporal shortsightedness. Such was Hezekiah. Yet Baxter calls us to a farsightedness—a largeness of soul that "beholds all the earth and desires to know how it goes with the cause and with the servants of the Lord."

Let us not simply say, "As long as all is well in my lifetime."

Cultivate Farsighted Vision

Paul's desire for Timothy to appoint men who will teach others also likewise looks into the future. He, too, was farsighted. Remember this is the same letter in which he says, "The time of my departure is at hand." Therefore, he wants Timothy to train the next generation to think this way about gospel ministry.

The lesson for us is, *necessary to faithful gospel ministry is an investment in the next generation of gospel ministers.*

This should translate into very concrete realities in our weekly lives. This is a responsibility the church shares corporately, but it will require of you a very definite investment of time, energy, and purpose.

Invest in the Next Gospel Generation

What will this look like? Let me suggest four possibilities. First, devote yourself to faithful gospel ministry, especially the ministry of the Word. The best way to train men to faithfully preach the gospel is to faithfully preach the gospel. William Perkins wrote, "So, let every minister both in his teaching and in his conversation work *in such a way* that he honors his calling, *so that* he may attract others to share his love for it."

Second, pay attention to the young men of various ages in your congregation. Notice how they receive your preaching. Notice how they process your preaching. Notice any deepening affections for God and his Word. Keep your eyes open.

Third, create contexts for the young men who catch your eye to practice and grow in their handling of the Word.

Fourth, and this must not go unsaid, pray very specifically for God to raise up the next generation of gospel ministers. Pray for your replacement but pray also for more than that. Pray with an eye, and a heart, toward the future and the continuing success of the gospel in the world, until Christ comes.

Editor's note: A version of this article was originally published at DesiringGod.org and is republished with permission.

Mike Bullmore served for 25 years as senior pastor of Crossway Community Church in Bristol, Wisconsin and is now teaching and training pastors in multiple venues.

Anticipating Your Reward

by Omar Johnson

"What then will we have?"
Pastor, have you ever pondered that question in your heart?

Your congregation grows slowly. Problems multiply rapidly. Colleagues enjoy bigger churches, better buildings, broader ministries. Culture drifts further from God and his Word yet prospers.

With all this, do you ponder, "What then will we have?"

The apostle Peter gives voice to our internal questioning. As he considered the cost of following Jesus and helping others to do the same, he asks Jesus, "What then will we have?" (Matt. 19:27)

Jesus responded,

> Truly, I say to you, in the new world, when the Son of Man will sit on his glorious throne, you who have followed me will also sit on twelve thrones, judging the twelve tribes of Israel. And everyone who has left houses or brothers or sisters or father or mother or children or lands, for my name's sake, will receive a

hundredfold and will inherit eternal life. (Matt. 19:28–29)

Ministry is hard. It normally involves some loss and lament. Jesus never denied this, but he also promised that they "will receive a hundredfold and will inherit eternal life."

Amidst the hardships and difficulties of ministry, Jesus's promise meant to propel Peter—and us—to keep going.

How does anticipating your reward help you in ministry?

Anticipating Your Rewards Keeps You Focused

Rewards are coming, but they're not the rewards we are tempted to want. After giving twenty-plus hours to sermon preparation, we want a large and attentive congregation who is arrested by our every word.

Does your heart sink like mine does when you step into the auditorium and there are more empty seats than full ones? When the person you hoped would be most moved by the message is absent? When the point you thought was going to hit home falls flat?

These disappointments easily lead to a Sunday afternoon somberness which then deepens into the Monday morning blues. Quiet quitting becomes a viable option. "Is this all really worth it?"

Pastor, the answer is yes. But we must remember what Jesus said the real reward is. He didn't promise us a full church. He didn't guarantee the full attention or appreciation of our members. He definitely didn't promise fame.

Instead, Jesus promised that *everyone* who follows him will inherit eternal life.

Don't focus on the rewards that were never promised to you. Focus on the ones that were promised.

Anticipating Your Rewards Keeps You Faithful

Faithfulness can feel like an underwhelming goal. It isn't driven by metrics or statistics, which leaves it feeling insignificant. After all, the world values production far more than loyal allegiance and perseverance.

Sometimes even church culture presents faithfulness like something akin to a participation trophy in sports. It's reserved for the losers who don't have the talent to make it big. Compelled to say something nice about them, we offer up a meager "Oh, yeah, they're . . . faithful."

But faithfulness is precious to the Lord.

Take the apostle Paul, who says the one thing that's required of pastors is that they be found faithful (1 Cor. 4:2).

Consider Jesus who says that heavenly rewards are reserved for those who remain faithful to him. "Enter into the joy of the Lord" is the invitation extended only to the "good and faithful servant" (Matt. 25:23).

Faithfulness in ministry, like faithfulness in marriage, isn't always exciting. In fact, it often feels like a slog; a steady plodding; putting one foot in front of the other. There normally isn't anything flashy about laboring in the Word and laboring to love people in the ways the Lord commanded.

Nonetheless, faithfulness is the goal. Faithfulness means refusing to tamper with God's Word or take any shortcuts—even if they seem to be surer, quicker paths to success (2 Cor. 4:1–2).

Faithfulness involves embracing your role as an undershepherd, and lovingly and tenderly shepherding those under your care with integrity. God has promised that when the Chief Shepherd appears, only then will you receive the unfading crown of glory (1 Pet. 5:1–4).

Faithfulness endures suffering: things like unjustified character attacks, unsolicited criticisms, unkind treatment. These things aren't confined to year one of ministry either. Some suffering from your ministry persists until the Lord returns or calls you home.

Brother pastor, we must respond not with violence and vitriol, but with love and joy. Why? Because even if people hate us and exclude us and revile us and spurn our name as evil on account of our ministry in service to the Savior, we know our reward is great in heaven (Luke 6:22–23).

The saints of old endured long, hard struggles. Sometimes they were publicly exposed to affliction and mistreatment. Sometimes they lost homes and property. But they joyfully held fast to Jesus. They knew they had a better, abiding possession waiting for them if they continued faithfully following the Lord (Heb. 10:32–34).

"Therefore," the author of Hebrews instructs us, "do not throw away your confidence in the Lord." Do not turn away from following him or grow weary of pastoring in the way he's prescribed. God has guaranteed us a great reward that awaits us. When we have endured and have done the will of God, we will receive what has been promised (Heb. 10:35–36).

What then will we have? Everything. Jesus said so. And he always keeps his promises. We must keep pastoring, pastor. Our reward is coming.

Omar Johnson is the senior pastor of Temple Hills Baptist Church in Temple Hills, Maryland.

Building Healthy Churches

IS YOUR CHURCH HEALTHY?

9Marks exists to equip church leaders with a biblical vision and practical resources for displaying God's glory to the nations through healthy churches.

To that end, we want to help churches grow in nine marks of health that are often overlooked:

1. Expositional Preaching
2. Gospel Doctrine
3. A Biblical Understanding of Conversion and Evangelism
4. Biblical Church Membership
5. Biblical Church Discipline
6. A Biblical Concern for Discipleship and Growth
7. Biblical Church Leadership
8. A Biblical Understanding of the Practice of Prayer
9. A Biblical Understanding and Practice of Missions

At 9Marks, we write articles, books, book reviews, and an online journal. We host conferences, record interviews and produce other resources to equip churches to display God's glory.

Visit our website to find content in **40+ languages** and sign up to receive our free online journal. See a complete list of our other language websites here:
9marks.org/about/international-efforts

9marks.org

www.ingramcontent.com/pod-product-compliance
Lightning Source LLC
Chambersburg PA
CBHW051119230426
43667CB00014B/2645